The Wesleyan Way

LEADER GUIDE

The Wesleyan Way

Book
Presents the beliefs and practices of Wesleyan Christianity in eight
chapters, through story and Scripture, for individual or group use.
978-1-4267-6756-2

DVD
Features inspiring and moving interviews with eight Christian leaders
who tell their faith stories. Interviews are about ten minutes long.
978-1-4267-6758-6

Leader Guide
Gives leaders everything they need to organize and run a group to
study The Wesleyan Way in eight sessions. Includes pre-class planning,
scheduling options, activities, and discussion questions for Scripture,
book, and DVD.
978-1-4267-6757-9

For more information, go to www.TheWesleyanWay.com.

SCOTT J. JONES

The Wesleyan Way

A Faith That Matters

Leader Guide
by Jessica Kelley

Abingdon Press

Nashville

THE WESLEYAN WAY: A FAITH THAT MATTERS
Leader Guide

ISBN 978-1-4267-6757-9

This Leader Guide includes quoted material from *The Wesleyan Way: A Faith That Matters*, by Scott J. Jones, copyright © 2013 by Abingdon Press.

Scripture quotations unless noted otherwise are from the Common English Bible. Copyright © 2011 by the Common English Bible. All rights reserved. Used by permission. www.CommonEnglishBible.com.

Scripture quotations marked NRSV are from the New Revised Standard Version of the Bible, copyright 1989, Division of Christian Education of the National Council of the Churches of Christ in the United States of America. Used by permission. All rights reserved.

Scripture quotation fro... The Authorized (King James) Version. Rights in the Authorized the United Kingdom are vested in the Crown. Reproduced by permission of the Crown's patentee, Cambridge University Press.

Scripture quotations marked NIV are taken from the Holy Bible, New International Version®, NIV®. Copyright © 1973, 1978, 1984, 2011 by Biblica, Inc.TM Used by permission of Zondervan. All rights reserved worldwide. www.zondervan.com. The "NIV" and "New International Version" are trademarks registered in the United States Patent and Trademark Office by Biblica, Inc.TM

Library of Congress Cataloging-in-Publication applied for.

13 14 15 16 17 18 19 20 21 22—10 9 8 7 6 5 4 3 2 1

MANUFACTURED IN THE UNITED STATES OF AMERICA

Contents

To the Group Leader

Today's culture is full of extremes, with people polarized on many social and political issues. People are often polarized to religious extremes as well—liberal and conservative, with no in-between. Anyone in the middle is seen to be apathetic, disengaged, or simply humdrum. The Wesleyan Way of salvation offers an alternative, occupying what some have called "the extreme center." Wesleyan Christianity is a passionate and engaged faith tradition that avoids extremes and seeks to love and serve all people in Jesus' name.

The world needs this extreme center, but the sad truth is that many Christians—even members of churches in the Wesleyan traditions—don't know much about the beliefs and practices that are central to the Wesleyan Way. This study aims to engage Christians in a deeper exploration of the historic and dynamic Wesleyan tradition, so they can grow in faith, live their faith, and share this faith with others.

Study participants will read *The Wesleyan Way* book by Scott Jones, one chapter for each of the study's eight sessions. The book, expressed in simple, contemporary terms, gives an excellent overview of John Wesley's theology and the Wesleyan practice of reading and applying Scripture.

Participants will meet as a group once a week for eight weeks to discuss and apply their book and Bible reading. At each meeting they will view one of eight videos on the DVD. The videos feature interviews with eight Christian leaders, including Scott J. Jones, sharing some of their personal stories of coming to faith and living out the Wesleyan Way in their own lives and churches.

This leader guide is designed to help you, as group leader, engage participants with what they have read in the book and Bible and viewed on the DVD. It provides suggestions for planning, structuring, and running the group sessions so participants get the most from the materials and from each other. The guide includes a session plan for each week, highlighting key points from the book, Bible, and DVD, with discussion questions and activities. These questions and activities will help participants bring head, heart, and hands together for a holistic exploration of each session's primary theme.

You and the group members will also want to visit the Wesleyan Way website, www.TheWesleyanWay.com. There, you'll find samples, documents, and short videos for enrichment before or after group sessions.

Session Themes

1. Following Christ Is a Way of Life (The Christian Life)
   This session emphasizes that salvation is more than a "Get Out of Hell Free" card, but a call to live fully and radically as a follower of Christ, loving God and loving our neighbors with the whole of our being.

2. Love Ultimately Wins (Who God Is)
   This session explores what we can and cannot know about God, and the ways in which we learn about and grow to know God personally.

3. It's a Good World with Issues (Human Potential and Sin)
   This session discusses the nature of humanity as created good, in God's image, and yet with an innate and strong tendency toward sin.

4. Turn Your Life Around with Grace (The Gift and Power of Grace)
   This session introduces a Wesleyan understanding of the various forms of grace God gives—prevenient, convincing, justifying, and sanctifying—and how we respond to this gift.

5. You Are Not Alone (Following Christ in Community)
   This session examines six "means of grace," or practices through which we actively respond to and grow in God's grace, often and preferably in community with other believers also on the journey.

6. Transform Yourself and the World (Spiritual Maturity)
   This session challenges participants to cultivate virtues emphasized in Scripture, living holy and humble lives, viewing people of every status with love, not judgment.

7. Invite Others on the Journey (Evangelism for Everyone)
   This session focuses on the sometimes-scary topic of evangelism, not keeping the grace we've experienced to ourselves but sharing our stories by inviting others to experience Christ for themselves.

8. Christ No Matter What (Hope in Light of the Unknown)
   This session concludes the exploration of the Wesleyan Way by acknowledging

the unanswerable questions in life and faith—why bad things happen, what happens after we die, who goes to heaven, and what will happen at the end of the world—and emphasizing our hope in Christ, no matter what.

Session Plans

Each session in this leader guide contains six elements—one designed for your personal use and the others to help you lead the group sessions.

Before Class

This section helps you as the leader to look at your own preconceived notions about the topic at hand. Being aware of your own beliefs and experiences related to the topic will help you be more open to the different perspectives participants may bring to the discussion. You do not need to share this section with your group unless you are comfortable doing so and feel that it enhances the session.

Welcome

Start class with a greeting and prayer. Consider singing together the hymns highlighted at the end of the book chapters, which are available in most hymnals. Jump right in with the provided icebreaker question to get participants thinking about the day's topic.

Bible Study and Discussion

Each session discusses two passages (or one longer passage) from Scripture related to the day's topic. Some of these Scriptures are mentioned or explored in the book chapters, and some are not. The full text of these passages (Common English Bible translation) is reprinted in the leader's guide, so you do not have to juggle multiple books during the session. Invite participants to volunteer to read the passages aloud, and then discuss the passages using the five questions provided. Space has been provided at three points in each session of this leader guide, so you can jot your own notes or additional questions you might want to ask.

Video Study and Discussion

Show the video for that session. The leaders interviewed in these videos will introduce themselves, so no introduction is required. Watch the video, and then discuss the leader's comments using the five questions provided or any other questions you have jotted in the space provided.

NOTES

Activity

This portion of the session is designed to help participants internalize the lessons of the day by processing ideas or practicing a Wesleyan behavior individually, with a partner, or with a smaller group within the class. The goal of these activities is mainly the experience of the assignment itself, though you should allow a few minutes for participants to debrief the experience or share their results with the group, if they so desire. Most of these activities require a small amount of simple preparation by you as the leader—usually the photocopying of activity pages and preparing them for your group.

Book Study and Discussion

After processing the week's topic through Scripture and the video, turn to the book chapter for that week and discuss the material in light of the other insights that have emerged. Use the five questions provided and any other questions you have jotted in the space provided. Short excerpts from the book have been reprinted in the leader guide as a reference for you to help fuel the discussion. These excerpts should not be considered an answer key; instead, make sure participants feel free to give their insights on the topic without being limited to a certain paragraph from the book.

Hymns (Optional)

Scott Jones closes each chapter of the student book with a hymn, most of them by Charles Wesley. To show the power of the original hymns and their application to our lives today, the hymns are presented in two versions: the traditional lyrics and a contemporary rephrasing, written by author and songwriter Jenny Youngman. Your group may choose to sing the hymns, recite them together, or simply use them for individual reading and reflection at home.

Faith Stories (Optional)

In addition to the eight video presentations that you'll use in the group, the DVD includes some short "faith stories" profiling people whose faith has helped them through difficult circumstances. Each session plan gives the title and description of a faith story that could be used effectively that week, if you would like to provide your group with an extra activity.

Suggested Time Allotments

The session breakdown here is only a guide—with a couple of options—for how long to spend on each element of the study. Some discussions may be very fruitful and need more time; others might be less fruitful, allowing more time for the next component.

	60-minute session	90-minute session
Welcome/Icebreaker	3 min.	5 min.
Bible Study and Discussion	15 min.	25 min.
Video Study and Discussion	15 min.	25 min.
Activity	7 min.	10 min.
Book Study and Discussion	20 min.	25 min.

Tips for Facilitating a Fruitful Discussion

- Create a friendly, open environment by offering coffee or snacks. If your schedule allows, build in buffer time to allow for the mingling and conversations that happen before and after class.

- Distribute books at least one week prior to the first group meeting, so participants can get a sense of the topics at hand and to read the first chapter.

- Express the expectation that participants read each chapter before class, but do not shame participants who do not. They can still gain much from and contribute to the discussion, and pressuring them to fake having read the material will hurt the authenticity of the discussion.

- Read through the leader guide for each week's session prior to reading the book chapter. You may notice things or gain insights that will be helpful for the discussion as you read. Read the Scripture passages and watch the video in advance as well, so you can make note of any additional questions you'd like to ask or observations you'd like to make.

- Allow time to think about the "Before Class" questions and to prepare any necessary materials for the session's activity.

- Let participants know they are free to disagree with the material presented, while still clarifying elements that are considered "essentials" of the Wesleyan tradition.

- Allow participants to reflect and respond to questions before offering your perspective or pointing them to a particular verse of Scripture or page of the book.

- Feel free to move on to the next question if a passage or activity does not resonate with your group or produce fruitful discussion.

1.

Following Christ Is a Way of Life

Session Summary

The word *salvation* sometimes has been misused by Christians and misunderstood by others. Yet, like many other words found in the Bible, it is best to keep using it and to do so with as much clarity as possible. When talking about the Wesleyan Way of salvation, one should keep in mind what Jesus said to many people whom he met. For many of them, salvation was about healing them of the brokenness in their lives. For some this meant physical healing. For others it was restoring broken relationships. For still others it meant life after death, in paradise. One way of explaining it is to say that salvation is *from* all the bad things in life, and salvation is *for* true happiness, joy, and meaning.

Salvation is more than membership in a church, although church membership is part of it. Salvation is more than a family affiliation, though one's family and upbringing may influence our path. People enter the Christian life in a variety of ways, but salvation is a lifelong journey. Once someone has entered into the Christian life, that person has been saved but is still being saved. Christians should understand that God has not finished with them just because they have entered into a saving relationship. All of us are sinners, and it takes a lifetime to become the kind of people God intends us to be.

Before Class

This session addresses deep questions about the basics of our faith, including questions that can carry some cultural baggage. Controversial issues may come up in your class discussion, so it is helpful to think beforehand about what you consider the essentials of your faith.

1. Why are you a Christian? What does being a Christian mean to you?

2. What is your feeling about the word *saved* and what it takes to "be saved"?

Welcome

Start class with a word of greeting and prayer. Consider singing the hymn that closes the week's chapter, "O for a Thousand Tongues to Sing."

Icebreaker question: What is your reaction to roadside billboards that say things such as "If you died tonight, where would you spend eternity?" (Responses might include the ethics and efficacy of fear tactics, the concept of heaven and hell, and the question of who can be saved and how.)

Bible Study and Discussion

Read the following passages from the Torah and Jesus' adaptation of it in Matthew.

Leviticus 19:11-18

You must not steal nor deceive nor lie to each other. ¹²You must not swear falsely by my name, desecrating your God's name in doing so; I am the LORD. ¹³You must not oppress your neighbors or rob them. Do not withhold a hired laborer's pay overnight. ¹⁴You must not insult a deaf person or put some obstacle in front of a blind person that would cause them to trip. Instead, fear your God; I am the LORD. ¹⁵You must not act unjustly in a legal case. Do not show favoritism to the poor or deference to the great; you must judge your fellow Israelites fairly. ¹⁶Do not go around slandering your people. Do not stand by while your neighbor's blood is shed; I am the LORD. ¹⁷You must not hate your fellow Israelite in your heart. Rebuke your fellow Israelite strongly, so you don't become responsible for his sin. ¹⁸You must not take revenge nor hold a grudge against any of your people; instead, you must love your neighbor as yourself; I am the LORD.

Deuteronomy 6:1-9

Now these are the commandments, the regulations, and the case laws that the LORD your God commanded me to teach you to follow in the land you are entering to possess, ²so that you will fear the LORD your

God by keeping all his regulations and his commandments that I am commanding you—both you and your sons and daughters—all the days of your life and so that you will lengthen your life. ³Listen to them, Israel! Follow them carefully so that things will go well for you and so that you will continue to multiply exactly as the Lord, your ancestors' God, promised you, in a land full of milk and honey.

⁴Israel, listen! Our God is the LORD! Only the LORD!

⁵Love the LORD your God with all your heart, all your being, and all your strength. ⁶These words that I am commanding you today must always be on your minds. ⁷Recite them to your children. Talk about them when you are sitting around your house and when you are out and about, when you are lying down and when you are getting up. ⁸Tie them on your hand as a sign. They should be on your forehead as a symbol. ⁹Write them on your house's doorframes and on your city's gates.

Matthew 22:34-40

³⁴When the Pharisees heard that Jesus had left the Sadducees speechless, they met together. ³⁵One of them, a legal expert, tested him. ³⁶"Teacher, what is the greatest commandment in the Law?" ³⁷He replied, *"You must love the Lord your God with all your heart, with all your being,* and with all your mind. ³⁸This is the first and greatest commandment. ³⁹And the second is like it: *You must love your neighbor as you love yourself.* ⁴⁰All the Law and the Prophets depend on these two commands."

Questions
1. Describe the covenant between God and Israel as laid out in Deuteronomy 6:1-9.

2. The command to "love your neighbor as yourself" in Leviticus 19:18 is somewhat buried amid instructions about animal sacrifices and avoiding fortune-tellers. What do you notice about the immediate context of the command (Leviticus 19:11-18)?

3. Matthew 22:35 says the Pharisees were testing Jesus with a question. What do you think they expected him to say?

4. Deuteronomy 6:4, called the "Shema" (Hebrew for *listen*), is a central affirmation of the Jewish faith, so the Pharisees may well have agreed with Jesus that it is the

NOTES

greatest commandment. What point do you think Jesus was making by saying that the law from Leviticus 19:18 was a close second?

5. In the book chapter we're discussing this week, Scott Jones says, "The Wesleyan Way of salvation is an answer to questions about how to live well." Do you think Jesus' definition of the greatest and second-greatest commandments could be called a way of salvation?

My other thoughts and questions:

Video Study and Discussion

Today's video segment features Andy Nixon, pastor of The Loft, an innovative faith community launched out of The Woodlands Church in Texas. Andy talks about his own journey to faith after being raised in a nonreligious household, and how he has come to understand just how radical God's love for us is and the power of salvation in Christ.

Watch the video, then discuss the following questions:
1. Andy describes his journey of faith as one of finding answers. What questions do you think are essential to experiencing the saving grace of God?

2. Andy asks himself, "Do I really trust Christ? I mean, do I really? Do I really love my neighbor?" How do you know the answers to these questions? Can you know these things for sure?

3. What do you think the former mobster whom Andy met found so compelling about Christianity? Can you relate to his raw emotion and deep curiosity about salvation? Why or why not?

4. Is it hard for you to accept that God forgives even the worst of sinners? How does that most radical forgiveness make you feel about your own salvation?

5. Do you think Andy is right in saying that Christians love one another more than those outside the church? If love is the essential test of our faith, how do we measure up? Are there essentials of Christianity we should expect of outsiders before bringing them into the fold?

My other thoughts and questions:

Activity: Essentials and Nonessentials

Supplies needed: photocopies of the list on the next page; plus scissors, envelopes, or paper clips.

The Wesleyan Way avoids some of the most contentious and divisive issues among Christians and focuses on the basic message of the Bible. Wesley seemed fond of a saying that is commonly attributed to St. Augustine (though its origin is disputed): "In essentials, unity; in non-essentials, liberty; in all things, charity." The difficult thing is that Christians tend to disagree about what beliefs and values should be considered essential.

For this activity, the class should break into groups of no more than five people each, and sort the paper strips provided into two categories: essential and nonessential. Essentials are those beliefs and values on which you think Christians should agree, and nonessentials are those on which you think Christians can "agree to disagree." Give groups five minutes to complete the task, then share and compare how groups categorized the ideas.

Essentials and Nonessentials

Make a copy of this page for every two to five people in your class, and cut them into strips along the dotted lines. Use envelopes or paper clips to keep each set of strips together to hand out to groups. Feel free to make additional strips with ideas not included on this page—things that might be current topics of debate in the news or in your particular congregation.

The Trinity	Abortion and euthanasia
Jesus' virgin birth	God's creation of the universe
Prayer in public schools	Heaven and hell
God's omnipotence and omniscience	Caring for the poor
Jesus' atoning death	Jesus' dual nature as human and divine
Loving our neighbors	Scripture as inspired by God
Evolution	Human sinfulness
The power of prayer	The second coming of Christ
The death penalty	Homosexuality
Jesus' physical resurrection	The inerrancy of Scripture

Book Study and Discussion

The book chapter we read this week introduces the "Wesleyan Way of salvation," the good news of God's plan and purpose for all people. The discussion for the remainder of the class time should enhance participants' understanding of the Wesleyan perspective, while recognizing the value of participants' own reading of the Scriptures and experience as Christians. The passages reprinted below for your convenience should be considered references for the discussion, not an answer key for the questions provided.

1. Why are you a Christian? What does it mean to you to be a Christian?

    How can anyone dare to suggest that one way of life is best? To other people, especially those who have been Christians all their lives, it's obvious that following Jesus is the best way to live. But even those people sometimes wonder what following Jesus really means. If we truly followed Jesus with utmost seriousness and intentionality, what would it look like?

2. The word *salvation* can be a loaded term in discussions of religion. What does the term mean to you? What misconceptions of "salvation" have you seen or heard? How can we as Wesleyans help correct those misunderstandings?

    The Wesleyan Way describes Christianity as a journey of following Jesus toward the goal of loving God with all of our heart, mind, soul, and strength and loving our neighbors as ourselves. Christianity is often described as salvation. In the Wesleyan Way, salvation is a journey toward eternal happiness.

    The word *salvation* sometimes has been misused by Christians and misunderstood by others. Yet, as with many other words found in the Bible, it is best to keep using them and to do so with as much clarity as possible. When talking about the Wesleyan Way of salvation, one should keep in mind what Jesus said to many people whom he met. For many, salvation was about healing them of the brokenness in their lives. For some this meant physical healing. For others it was restoring broken relationships. For still others it meant life after death in paradise. One way of expressing this wide variety of meanings is to say that salvation is *from* all the bad things in life and *for* true happiness, joy, and truth.

3. Fellowship and connection are wonderful parts of living one's faith, but church membership and family affiliation by themselves do not make us Christians. What are some of the pros and cons of a tightly knit church community and a family united in faith?

> Salvation is more than membership in a church, though church membership is part of it. In some cases church membership doesn't appear to be much different from any other group affiliation or even a club membership. Churches, like clubs, have a purpose, attendance expectations, dues and requirements, and benefits that go along with membership. Some congregations have boiled down their understanding of salvation to "join our club—see what great benefits we offer!"

> Salvation is more than a family affiliation, though one's family and upbringing may influence our path. There is no doubt that our families shape many things about us. Some of those things are genetic. Others involve a complex web of relationships, values, and loyalties that constitute a family's identity. Thus, because religion is an expression of our highest and most sacred values and relationships, our families often shape our faith. In more traditional societies, one's experience of salvation is actually part of the family experience, and changing religions is unheard of.

4. It's no secret that different denominations within Christianity—and different people within each denomination—disagree on many issues related to belief and practice of the Christian faith. The "Essentials and Nonessentials" activity from this session may have revealed differences within your own group. What issues seem to be causing the most disagreement among Christians in your community? How can we learn to work together and love one another despite our differences?

> Scripture is authoritative for all Christians, but the differences within the Christian family show that we read this amazing, complex, and powerful book in different ways. Each way of reading Scripture can lead to a different version of the Christian life.

> The Wesleyan Way of reading and interpreting the Bible avoids some of the most contentious and divisive issues among Christians and focuses on the basic message of the text.

What we will study in this book and DVD is the Wesleyan Way of following Jesus, as taught by John and Charles Wesley in their eighteenth-century movement. That movement sought the renewal of their church, the Church of England, but it eventually led to the formation of many different Wesleyan churches. The Wesleyan Way presented in this study relates to the official teaching of many of those groups. Those of us in the Wesleyan tradition don't always practice this way of life very well, but if you ask and look carefully, this is what we are trying to do when we are at our best.

5. Our salvation has implications for life on earth and life after death. What is the relationship between following Jesus on earth and living with him in heaven? How do we trust in eternal life to come without, as the saying goes, "being so heaven-minded that we're no earthly good"?

The ultimate goal of following Jesus is life forever with God. The short-term goal (the length of our lives here on earth) is having a life that matters. The Wesleyan Way teaches that God has created each person to live in relationship with him. People are happiest and most fulfilled when they acknowledge God as creator and Lord and when they seek to be the kind of men and women God intended.

Part of discipleship is our beliefs, or what we think is true about God, the world, and humanity. Part of discipleship is our behavior, always trying to do good. Part of discipleship is practicing spiritual disciplines such as prayer, worship, Bible study, and Holy Communion. Part of discipleship is being baptized into the body of Christ and participating as a member of Christ's church. Part of discipleship is discovering spiritual gifts and then using them in service for Christ. Part of discipleship is sharing faith with those who don't know Christ as Lord and Savior.

Meaning, purpose, and joy are best experienced by following Jesus Christ as Lord and Savior. Christians have a vision of how to live that is described as discipleship.

My other thoughts and questions:

NOTES

Faith Stories (Optional)

You may want to encourage your group to visit www.TheWesleyanWay.com. The site has information about the presenters, video clips from upcoming sessions, and links to more information about Wesleyan theology and heritage. There are additional short, personal video testimonies at TheWesleyanWay.com website and on your teaching DVD, under the heading "Faith Stories." You may want to spark conversation or wrap up the session with one of these short clips.

2.

Love Ultimately Wins

Session Summary

Responding to the questions "Is there a God?" and "Who is God?" makes it easier to answer the question about the meaning and purpose of human life. If there is a supreme being, and that being either made the world or controls it, then our place in the universe as humans becomes much clearer. If there is no God and the universe is some sort of cosmic accident, then some other biologically driven purpose might be proposed. Some have suggested that we are wired for survival of our species, and that is the highest good. Various religions suggest that pleasing the supreme being or fulfilling that being's intention is the answer.

Within the Christian tradition, theologians and philosophers have sometimes offered arguments to prove the existence of God. However, rarely has anyone been converted to Christianity by arguments alone. Rather, theologians and philosophers have offered such arguments to show that the faith commitments people have do in fact make sense and are rationally defensible. The Bible never offers any proof for the existence of God. Instead, its opening verse assumes there is a God and describes what that God has done.

Before Class

Belief in a supreme being is among the most basic elements of faith, but that doesn't mean such a belief is simple. It's impossible to understand completely and very hard even to explain our belief in God. Think about these questions:

1. What proof do you see of God? Do you believe there can be convincing evidence for or against belief in God?

2. If you were to try to convince an atheist of God's existence, what would you say?

Welcome

Start class with a word of greeting and prayer. Consider singing the hymn that closes the week's chapter, "Maker in Whom We Live."

Icebreaker question: Is there any way to prove God's existence?

Bible Study and Discussion

Read the following passages from Genesis 1 and John 1, and answer the questions that follow.

Genesis 1:1-13

When God began to create the heavens and the earth—[2]the earth was without shape or form, it was dark over the deep sea, and God's wind swept over the waters—[3]God said, "Let there be light." And so light appeared. [4]God saw how good the light was. God separated the light from the darkness. [5]God named the light Day and the darkness Night.

There was evening and there was morning: the first day.

[6]God said, "Let there be a dome in the middle of the waters to separate the waters from each other." [7]God made the dome and separated the waters under the dome from the waters above the dome. And it happened in that way. [8]God named the dome Sky.

There was evening and there was morning: the second day.

[9]God said, "Let the waters under the sky come together into one place so that the dry land can appear." And that's what happened. [10]God named the dry land Earth, and he named the gathered waters Seas. God saw how good it was. [11]God said, "Let the earth grow plant life: plants yielding seeds and fruit trees bearing fruit with seeds inside it, each according to its kind throughout the earth." And that's what happened. [12]The earth produced plant life: plants yielding seeds, each according to its kind, and trees bearing fruit with seeds inside it, each according to its kind. God saw how good it was.

[13]There was evening and there was morning: the third day.

John 1:1-14

In the beginning was the Word
   and the Word was with God
   and the Word was God.
[2]The Word was with God in the beginning.
[3]Everything came into being through the Word,
   and without the Word
   nothing came into being.
What came into being
   [4]through the Word was life,
   and the life was the light for all people.
[5]The light shines in the darkness,
   and the darkness doesn't extinguish the light.

[6]A man named John was sent from God. [7]He came as a witness to testify concerning the light, so that through him everyone would believe in the light. [8]He himself wasn't the light, but his mission was to testify concerning the light.

[9]The true light that shines on all people
   was coming into the world.
[10]The light was in the world,
   and the world came into being through the light,
     but the world didn't recognize the light.
[11]The light came to his own people,
   and his own people didn't welcome him.
[12]But those who did welcome him,
   those who believed in his name,
   he authorized to become God's children,
     [13]born not from blood
      nor from human desire or passion,
     but born from God.
[14]The Word became flesh
   and made his home among us.
We have seen his glory,
   glory like that of a father's only son,
     full of grace and truth.

NOTES

Questions

1. Both of these passages talk about "the beginning." What does John 1 add to the picture of Creation painted by Genesis 1?

2. What can we learn about God through these two passages? What characteristics of God do you see? Do you see God's love expressed in these passages?

3. The "Word" in John 1 is interpreted to refer to and suggest that Christ is the essential message or mind of God. What does the metaphor of the Word tell you about the nature of God and who Jesus is?

4. John 1 is seen as alluding to a Trinitarian understanding of God. How does the Trinity help you understand God?

5. Both of these passages use grand, dramatic, poetic language to describe God's work in the world. Does reading the passages enhance or complicate your faith? Do you take away any specifics about God from them or a more general impression of God's grandeur?

My other thoughts and questions:

Video Study and Discussion

Today's video segment features Adam Hamilton, pastor of The Church of the Resurrection, in Leawood, Kansas. Adam explains how the real test of faith is not in intellectual arguments or understanding, but in showing love to others.

Watch the video, then discuss the following questions:

1. Adam came to know God as a result of a personal invitation to church, ongoing attendance in worship there, and reading the Bible himself. What elements have you found to be most powerful for learning about God?

2. Do you think it is harder for what Adam calls "thinking people" to come to faith in God? How can a tendency toward intellectual and analytical thinking both hinder and enhance faith in God?

3. Do you think it is true that caring about people, and listening to their stories, makes a stronger case for faith than intellectually defending our beliefs? What examples have you seen of this? Is a caring relationship enough, or do we need to explain our beliefs at some point?

4. How do you tend to define a "strong Christian"? Is it someone who knows many Bible verses by heart, prays an hour day, and can explain theological principles and the reasons he or she believes; or is it someone who genuinely cares about other people? Do you apply these same criteria when looking at your own spiritual life?

5. If love matters more than belief, what does that say about our differences of understanding about God or any other theological concept?

My other thoughts and questions:

Activity: The Blind Men and the Elephant

Supplies needed: a photocopy of the next page; scissors.

There is an old legend that is useful for thinking about how we understand God. According to this legend, four blind men were walking together and came across an elephant. Trying to picture this animal they'd encountered, each man came closer and felt the elephant, describing it to his friends. The first man stood by the elephant's side and felt the broad, firm expanse. "An elephant is like a wall," he told his friends. The second man held the elephant's tail and said, "No, an elephant is like a rope." The third man felt the animal's massive leg and said, "An elephant is like a strong tree trunk." The last man wrangled the elephant's thick, flexible trunk and said, "No, an elephant is like a snake."

The story illustrates how difficult it is to get a complete picture of something with a limited vantage point.

For this activity, the class should break into four groups. Give each group one of the Scriptures listed on the handout. Ask each group to describe how they would imagine God if that particular passage of Scripture were their only source of information about God.

The Blind Men and the Elephant

Make a copy of this page and cut along the dotted lines to make four cards. Give one to each group.

Genesis 2:4*b*-23

Deuteronomy 9:13-29

Psalm 103

Luke 15:11-32

Book Study and Discussion

The book chapter we read this week explores the various ways we understand God, while at the same time emphasizing that we cannot know all the details about God, nor do we need to. Love is the most important thing to understand about God and about how God wants us to live. The discussion for the remainder of the class time should enhance participants' understanding of the Wesleyan perspective, while recognizing the value of participants' own reading of the Scriptures and experience as Christians. The passages reprinted below for your convenience should be considered references for the discussion, not an answer key for the questions provided.

1. How does our understanding of God determine how we live? What misunderstandings of God might lead us to live in fear or harm others?

   Answering the questions "Is there a God?" and "Who is God?" makes it easier to draw some conclusions about the meaning and purpose of human life. If there is a supreme being who either made the world or controls it, then our place in the universe as humans becomes clearer. If there is no God and the universe is a cosmic accident, then some other biologically driven purpose might be proposed. Some have said we are wired for survival of our species and that is the highest good. Various religions suggest that pleasing or fulfilling the intention of a supreme being is the answer.

2. How important is it to be able to defend your faith rationally? Does having proof of God help you personally to have a stronger faith? Does it help you share your faith with non-Christians?

   My experience is that no one has ever been converted to Christianity by an argument. Rather, the arguments of theologians and philosophers seem most useful after the fact, showing that the faith commitments of believers do in fact make sense and are rationally defensible.

   The Bible itself never offers any proof for the existence of God. Instead, its opening verse assumes there is a God and describes what that God has done. "When God began to create the heavens and the earth . . ." (Genesis 1:1).

For Christians, the answer to the four religious questions is ultimately settled by faith—a commitment to live in this way because it fits. It makes sense. It is right. According to Hebrews 11:1, "Faith is the reality of what we hope for, the proof of what we don't see." Faith is our decision that God is real and that we want to live our lives in relationship with God.

3. John Wesley points out that God is called "holy, righteous, wise; but not holiness, righteousness, or wisdom in the abstract, as he is said to be love." What does it mean to you that love trumps all of God's other attributes?

   There are many things that can be said about God's nature and being. Philosophers and theologians often speak of God's attributes, using adjectives such as the following:

   Omnipresent—God is everywhere.
   Omnipotent—God is all-powerful.
   Omniscient—God is all-knowing.
   Sovereign—God rules the universe.
   Eternal—God has always existed, will never cease to exist, and is not subject to time.
   Wise—God knows the right thing to do.
   Holy—God is completely other and completely righteous

   John Wesley believed all these attributes to be true, but he regarded God's most important attribute—indeed, God's very definition—to be love. He makes a comment in his *Explanatory Notes Upon the New Testament* at 1 John 4:8:

   > God is often styled holy, righteous, wise; but not holiness, righteousness, or wisdom in the abstract, as he is said to be love; intimating that this is his darling, his reigning attribute, the attribute that sheds an amiable glory on all his other perfections.

4. The Bible can be considered the story of God's people throughout many centuries before and immediately following Jesus' earthly life. Do you see God's love evident throughout this story? Is God's love shown differently in different parts of the Bible? Is God's love shown differently in different parts of the Trinity?

God's call of Israel began with Abraham. God said to Abraham:

> "Leave your land, your family, and your father's household for the land that I will show you. I will make of you a great nation and will bless you. I will make your name respected, and you will be a blessing. I will bless those who bless you, those who curse you I will curse; all the families of earth will be blessed because of you."

This call began the special relationship that Abraham's descendants have had with God ever since. Abraham's son Isaac had a son named Jacob. After wrestling with God at the river Jabbok, Jacob was renamed Israel and his descendants were called Israelites. They went to Egypt and lived there for many years, ending up in slavery to the Egyptians.

The Exodus from slavery in Egypt was a defining moment for the Israelites. The Passover recalls God's miraculous actions to save them: God remembered his people and brought them out of slavery on a journey to a land of their own.

At Mount Sinai, God gave the law to the people of Israel and commanded them to obey. For Jews, the law comprises the first five books of the Bible. One of its most important verses is Deuteronomy 6:4-5 which says, "Hear, O Israel: The LORD is our God, the LORD alone. You shall love the LORD your God with all your heart, and with all your soul, and with all your might" (NRSV).

Despite the Israelites' misbehavior over many generations, God did not forsake them. He rescued them from slavery in the Exodus. He gave them a land "flowing with milk and honey." When they worshipped other gods, borrowing the practices of neighboring peoples, he sent them prophets to remind them that God wished them to be a holy people.

Part of their holiness was worshipping the Lord and only him. Another part was how they treated the poor, especially widows and orphans, who were the most vulnerable. The Israelites insisted that foreigners be welcomed and treated fairly. The prophets kept them focused on worship of the Lord and justice for all. Some of the prophets also looked forward to a future king of Israel who would redeem his people. Many passages from Isaiah and Malachi were later interpreted to be foretelling a Messiah.

5. John 13:35 says, "This is how everyone will know that you are my disciples, when you love each other." Is love what the church is known for today? Is it what your church is known for? Is it what you are known for? How can we—as individual Christians and collectively as the body of Christ—embody God's love today?

We have seen that God's very nature is love. God loves the world and God calls all human beings to love him and their neighbor. When we are baptized, we are baptized into Christ, into one body. A key New Testament metaphor for the church is as the body of Christ. Thus, if God is love, and Christ is God, then the church is the love of Christ embodied in the world. At its best, the church is a place where the Holy Spirit is both present and seen to be present. It shows God's love in its daily life through its words and actions. It is a loving community.

At its best, the church continues to do these things today. Thousands of churches feed the poor, welcome strangers, and help those suffering from natural disasters.

Yet the church is composed of human beings who are sinners. We are all too familiar with the many ways we fall short of truly embodying God's love. Nevertheless, loving and acting on that love remain the church's purpose and calling from God.

My other thoughts and questions:

Faith Stories (Optional)

There are additional short, personal video testimonies at TheWesleyanWay.com website and on your teaching DVD. You may want to spark conversation or wrap up the session the session with one of these short clips.

Adam: Bless the Schools (4:39)—Adam Hamilton describes the partnership that his congregation has begun with local schools in underserved areas of Kansas City. He lifts up the Wesleyan emphasis on care for the poor and access to education.

3.

It's a Good World with Issues

Session Summary

According to the Bible, humanity is created in the image of God. While human beings may share many physical characteristics with animals, we are primarily spirits like God. Also, God gave humanity dominion over the earth and its creatures. This is a huge responsibility! But the most important aspect of being created in the image of God is that we are capable of love. God is love, and we were created with the purpose of loving God and loving our neighbor as ourselves. When human beings are at our best, we love the Lord and each other very well.

Yet, the truth is that we don't live that way. While the creation is good and God's intentions are for us to love him and each other well, in practice we regularly and sometimes spectacularly violate God's plan for us. We have issues. Sin is a violation of God's intentions for us. We sin when we break God's commandments. We are sinners. We mess things up.

Genesis portrays humanity as deeply flawed right from the beginning. Whether you believe that Adam and Eve were real people in the ancient past or that the story of their disobedience is a true portrayal of all humanity, the account is fundamental to Christian teaching about sin. God commanded Adam not to eat of the tree of the knowledge of good and evil. The serpent tempted Eve, and she gave in even though she knew it was wrong. Then she offered the fruit to Adam, and he did what he knew violated God's rule. Christians have called this "original sin" because it is so fundamental to human nature.

Before Class

Our individual perspective on the good and evil in our world shapes the way we understand God and the way we interpret all the problems we see in the world around us, from human violence to natural disasters.

1. Do you believe people are inherently good or inherently sinful?

2. Does your answer to the first question apply even to people who commit heinous acts of evil, such as Adolf Hitler or Osama bin Laden?

Welcome

Start class with a word of greeting and prayer. Consider singing the hymn that closes the week's chapter, "After a Relapse into Sin," now generally called "Depth of Mercy."

Icebreaker question: It can be easy to focus on bad news. What signs of good do you see in the world around you? (Popular responses might include the beauty of nature and the love of family. Challenge participants to name something original and to not repeat answers, in order to identify as many positive signs as you can.)

Bible Study and Discussion

Read Psalms 8 and 51, and answer the questions that follow.

Psalm 8

> LORD, our Lord, how majestic
>   is your name throughout the earth!
>   You made your glory higher than heaven!
> 2From the mouths of nursing babies
>   you have laid a strong foundation
>   because of your foes,
>   in order to stop vengeful enemies.
> 3When I look up at your skies,
>   at what your fingers made—
>   the moon and the stars
>   that you set firmly in place—
>   4what are human beings
>   that you think about them;

what are human beings
    that you pay attention to them?
5You've made them only slightly less than divine,
    crowning them with glory and grandeur.
6You've let them rule over your handiwork,
    putting everything under their feet—
        7all sheep and all cattle,
        the wild animals too,
        8the birds in the sky,
        the fish of the ocean,
        everything that travels the pathways of the sea.
9Lord, our Lord, how majestic is your name throughout the earth!

Psalm 51

Have mercy on me, God, according to your faithful love!
    Wipe away my wrongdoings according to your great compassion!
2Wash me completely clean of my guilt;
    purify me from my sin!
3Because I know my wrongdoings,
    my sin is always right in front of me.
4I've sinned against you—you alone.
    I've committed evil in your sight.
That's why you are justified when you render your verdict,
    completely correct when you issue your judgment.
5Yes, I was born in guilt, in sin,
    from the moment my mother conceived me.
6And yes, you want truth in the most hidden places;
    you teach me wisdom in the most secret space.

7Purify me with hyssop and I will be clean;
    wash me and I will be whiter than snow.
8Let me hear joy and celebration again;
    let the bones you crushed rejoice once more.
9Hide your face from my sins;
    wipe away all my guilty deeds!
10Create a clean heart for me, God;
    put a new, faithful spirit deep inside me!
11Please don't throw me out of your presence;
    please don't take your holy spirit away from me.

NOTES

¹²Return the joy of your salvation to me
    and sustain me with a willing spirit.
¹³Then I will teach wrongdoers your ways,
    and sinners will come back to you.
¹⁴Deliver me from violence, God, God of my salvation,
    so that my tongue can sing of your righteousness.
¹⁵Lord, open my lips,
    and my mouth will proclaim your praise.
¹⁶You don't want sacrifices.
    If I gave an entirely burned offering,
    you wouldn't be pleased.
¹⁷A broken spirit is my sacrifice, God.
    You won't despise a heart, God, that is broken and crushed.
¹⁸Do good things for Zion by your favor.
    Rebuild Jerusalem's walls.
¹⁹Then you will again want sacrifices of righteousness—
    entirely burned offerings and complete offerings.
        Then bulls will again be sacrificed on your altar.

Questions

1. What does Psalm 8 tell you about humanity? How is it a hymn of praise to God when it also seems to praise humanity?

2. Psalm 51 is said to be David's lament after his adultery with Bathsheba and murder of her husband, Uriah, but what can it tell us about the nature of all humans?

3. Compare verse 5 of each psalm. What truth about humanity is revealed in these two contrasting statements?

4. What elements of good do you see in Psalm 51? How can positive things come out of confession and lament?

5. Can you identify with the sorrow and regret of Psalm 51? Can you identify with Psalm 8:5-6 as easily? How might you live differently if you took those verses (Psalm 8:5-6) to heart?

My other thoughts and questions:

Video Study and Discussion

Today's video segment features Olu Brown, leader of Impact Church, an innovative congregation in Atlanta, Georgia. Growing up in—and serving in—communities that struggle from a lack of resources, Olu emphasizes the importance of being a countercultural, prophetic voice to help alleviate suffering and oppression in our world.

Watch the video, then discuss the following questions:

1. David's lament in Psalm 51 was a result of the prophet Nathan making David aware of his wrongdoing. Olu says we need to be Nathans, speaking truth to power. What keeps us from calling out powerful people and organizations on their wrongdoing?

2. Olu points out that even nonreligious people want to be part of movements to help others and address social issues. What does that say to you about human nature and the role of religion?

3. What does it mean to be stewards of the earth? Do you agree with Olu that stewardship or "dominion" over the earth includes being responsible for helping people and defending human rights?

4. What methods do we have for isolating ourselves from the problems in our world? How can we break down these barriers so we can see the struggles of our fellow human beings and build relationships with them?

5. What would it mean today for the last to be first and the first to be last? Which are you? How do we play a role in upending the world's order of things?

My other thoughts and questions:

Activity: Facing Our Issues

Supplies needed: a photocopy of the next page; scissors.

It is easy, as Jesus said, to point out the speck in others' eyes and ignore the plank in our own; that is, to call out other people's sins and shortcomings while overlooking our own. It is easy to name the big, obvious problems in our world, such as violent crime and global hunger. In this activity, take a look at the less obvious issues that may reflect "quiet sins" in our own lives.

Divide the class into six groups. Give each group one of the cards copied and cut from below. Have the groups discuss the problem named on their card. What evidence do you see of this issue in your community? How might you be part of this problem? How can you be part of the solution?

Facing Our Issues

Photocopy this page and cut along the dotted lines to make six cards. Give one to each group.

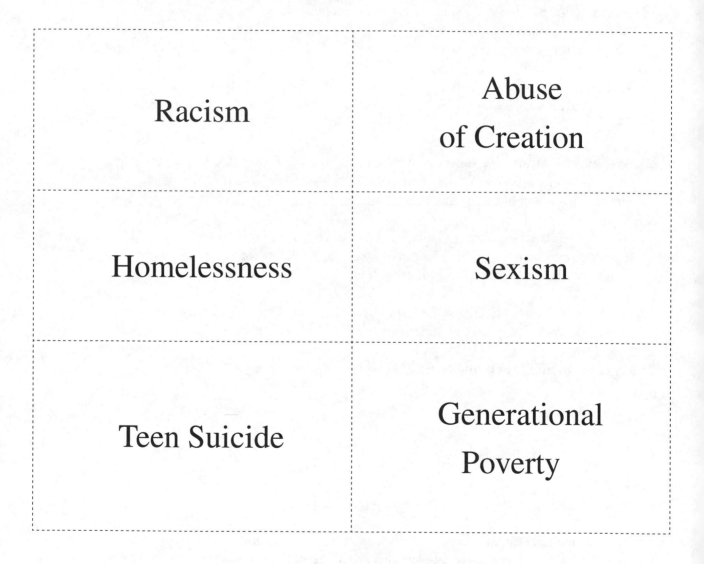

Racism	Abuse of Creation
Homelessness	Sexism
Teen Suicide	Generational Poverty

Book Study and Discussion

The book chapter we read this week addresses how good and bad coexist in our world. God created all things good, and yet we have "issues" that continually challenge and tarnish that goodness. The discussion for the remainder of the class time should enhance participants' understanding of the Wesleyan perspective, while recognizing the value of participants' own reading of the Scriptures and experience as Christians. The passages reprinted below for your convenience should be considered references for the discussion, not an answer key for the questions provided.

1. What are the implications of humans being created "in God's image"? What does that tell us about ourselves, and what does it tell us about God?

> The third primary message of Genesis 1 is humanity's special place in God's creation. . . . When Wesleyans discuss humanity, we talk about three different ways in which we are created in God's image. The first is that, like God, we are a spirit. There are those who wish to treat humanity as more closely related to the other animals, but Christianity puts us just a little below God. . . . Thus, while human beings may share many physical characteristics with animals, we are primarily spirits like God.

> The second way we are created in God's image is also expressed in Psalm 8 and Genesis 1. God gave humanity dominion over the earth and its creatures. This is a huge responsibility! As our numbers have increased, our impact on the earth has increased and not always for the better. We have the opportunity to do a better job of caring for the world God loves, and our actions as Christians should always take environmental concerns into account. We are responsible.

> The third and most important aspect of our being created in the image of God is that we are capable of love. God is love, and we were created with the purpose of loving God and loving our neighbor as ourselves. When human beings are at our best, we love the Lord and each other.

2. How should the doctrine of humans being created in God's image affect the way we treat other people and what it means to serve a God who values humanity?

> If humans are created in God's image, then every person is valuable in God's sight. The Old Testament commanded that the people of

NOTES

God should care for the poor, especially the widows and orphans who were the most vulnerable in society, and should welcome the alien and stranger into their communities.

Our care for the poor has developed into a commitment to human rights and human dignity, including our evolving commitment to the rights of women, who frequently have been subjected to discrimination and unequal treatment. Even parts of the Bible, reflecting the culture of the time in which it was written, have been used to violate the basic principle that all people are created in God's image. (p. 40 of *The Wesleyan Way* and following sections on slavery, diversity, and environmental justice)

3. How do you define original sin? What evidence do you see for it, and what does it mean for our potential as humans?

Genesis portrays humanity as deeply flawed right from the beginning. Whether you believe that Adam and Eve were real people in the ancient past or that the story of their disobedience is a metaphorical portrayal of all humanity, their story is fundamental to Christian teaching about sin. God commanded Adam not to eat from the tree of the knowledge of good and evil. The serpent tempted Eve and she gave in, even though she knew it was wrong. Then she offered the fruit to Adam, and he did what he knew violated God's rule.

We call their actions "original sin" because it is so fundamental to human nature. All human beings are sinners. Psalm 51 expresses David's deep confession of sin after committing adultery with Bathsheba, and in verse 5 he says, "Yes, I was born in guilt, in sin, from the moment my mother conceived me."

4. We are often more comfortable talking about other people's sin rather than our own. What sins do we most often overlook in ourselves? How does humility give us a better understanding of our own sinfulness?

I asked, "What should I preach about?" They replied, "Sin." When I asked what sins I should talk about, they named murder, theft, and other similar major crimes. I looked at the people in the room and realized that no one in the group was likely to have done any of those things. So I spent the rest of the lesson talking about racism, sexism, greed, ignoring the poor, adultery, and speeding. They got very uncomfortable as I hit closer to home.

When we take sin as seriously as the Bible does, we gain a greater humility. We acknowledge that we are flawed and have broken God's laws. (See Romans 2:1-3.)

Jesus tried to cultivate this attitude of humility in those he taught. Though Jesus had a lot in common with the Pharisees, he often used them as examples of self-righteous people who did not know their own need for God. (See Luke 18:10-14.) In our sinful ways, we human beings seek to justify ourselves. Following Jesus means focusing on our own sins first and being realistic about the ways in which sin has infected our thoughts, words, and deeds.

5. John Wesley talked about "natural conscience" and "prevenient (preventing) grace." Do people have an innate sense of right and wrong? How does God work in people who have experienced salvation in Christ and those who have not?

Wesleyans teach that God is in the business of saving sinners. God's grace has the power to end our disobedience and to shape our hearts to live according to God's purposes for us. However, God does not force us into a cure. Grace is offered to all and is available if we will accept the gift and use it. John Wesley said "No man living is entirely destitute of what is vulgarly called 'natural conscience.' But this is not natural; it is more properly termed 'preventing grace.' Every man has a greater or less measure of this. . . . So that no man sins because he has not grace, but because he does not use the grace which he hath. He sins because he does not use the grace which he hath." (*The Works of John Wesley*, ed. by W. Reginald Ward and Richard J. Heitzenrater; Abingdon Press, 2005; 3:207)

God's grace is actively helping all of us to address the problem of sin in our lives. For some people, addressing sin means learning that God loves them regardless of what they have done. For others, it means becoming aware of sin in their lives and the need to deal with it. . . . The Wesleyan Way is a journey in which God's grace works on us to overcome the power of sin in our lives and to become the people God intended from the beginning.

My other thoughts and questions:

Faith Stories (Optional)

There are additional short, personal video testimonies at TheWesleyanWay.com website and on your teaching DVD. You may want to spark conversation or wrap up the session the session with one of these short clips.

Rob: A Deeper Faith (4:45)—Rob's life was completely turned around after experiencing a heart attack in Sunday worship. His health scare led him to deeper questions about faith and purpose.

4.

Turn Your Life Around
with Grace

Session Summary

All of us have issues. We have problematic aspects of our lives that need to be addressed. All of us are sinners. The good news is that God loves us and is trying to heal us. We don't deserve that love—it is a gift that flows from God's very nature as our loving creator. That active love that seeks to shape our lives is called grace.

Wesleyan Christians believe that God's grace leads human beings from their brokenness to maturity, from sin to perfection. That journey is the way of salvation. But God does not force anyone to make the journey. God created humanity in God's own image, and part of God's nature includes free will. God did not create robots who were programmed to obedience; instead, all of us have the ability to obey or disobey.

In the same way, God's healing power does not overwhelm us. God loves us enough to allow us to reject his gift of love. God's grace is resistible. Yet, when we accept that grace and allow God to shape our hearts, minds, and lives, amazing things can happen.

Before Class

Discussions of sin and grace can raise powerful emotions, including regret, hurt, gratitude, or even doubt. Think about these questions before class to prepare yourself for the conversation ahead.

1. What sin in your own life makes you most aware of your need for grace?

NOTES

2. What was your experience of receiving God's grace? Was it a dramatic turnaround or a long, ongoing process?

3. Has anyone sinned against you so grievously that it is hard to imagine God extending grace to that person?

Welcome

Start class with a word of greeting and prayer. Consider singing the hymn that closes the week's chapter, "And Can It Be that I Should Gain."

Icebreaker question: What is the first thing that comes to your mind when I say the word *grace*? (Answers might include the hymn "Amazing Grace," a person named Grace, or an acrostic such as "God's Riches At Christ's Expense.")

Bible Study and Discussion

Read the following passages from Genesis 3 and Luke 15.

Genesis 3: 1-14, 21-24

The snake was the most intelligent of all the wild animals that the LORD God had made. He said to the woman, "Did God really say that you shouldn't eat from any tree in the garden?"

²The woman said to the snake, "We may eat the fruit of the garden's trees ³but not the fruit of the tree in the middle of the garden. God said, 'Don't eat from it, and don't touch it, or you will die.'"

⁴The snake said to the woman, "You won't die! ⁵God knows that on the day you eat from it, you will see clearly and you will be like God, knowing good and evil." ⁶The woman saw that the tree was beautiful with delicious food and that the tree would provide wisdom, so she took some of its fruit and ate it, and also gave some to her husband, who was with her, and he ate it. ⁷Then they both saw clearly and knew that they were naked. So they sewed fig leaves together and made garments for themselves.

⁸During that day's cool evening breeze, they heard the sound of the LORD God walking in the garden; and the man and his wife hid themselves

from the Lord God in the middle of the garden's trees. [9]The Lord God called to the man and said to him, "Where are you?"

[10]The man replied, "I heard your sound in the garden; I was afraid because I was naked, and I hid myself."

[11]He said, "Who told you that you were naked? Did you eat from the tree, which I commanded you not to eat?"

[12]The man said, "The woman you gave me, she gave me some fruit from the tree, and I ate."

[13]The Lord God said to the woman, "What have you done?!"

And the woman said, "The snake tricked me, and I ate. . . ."

[21]The Lord God made the man and his wife leather clothes and dressed them. [22]The Lord God said, "The human being has now become like one of us, knowing good and evil. Now so he doesn't stretch out his hand and take also from the tree of life and eat and live forever," [23]the Lord God sent him out of the garden of Eden to farm the fertile land from which he was taken. [24]He drove out the human. To the east of the garden of Eden, he stationed winged creatures wielding flaming swords to guard the way to the tree of life.

Luke 15: 11-32

[11]Jesus said, "A certain man had two sons. [12]The younger son said to his father, 'Father, give me my share of the inheritance.' Then the father divided his estate between them. [13]Soon afterward, the younger son gathered everything together and took a trip to a land far away. There, he wasted his wealth through extravagant living.

[14]"When he had used up his resources, a severe food shortage arose in that country and he began to be in need. [15]He hired himself out to one of the citizens of that country, who sent him into his fields to feed pigs. [16]He longed to eat his fill from what the pigs ate, but no one gave him anything. [17]When he came to his senses, he said, 'How many of my father's hired hands have more than enough food, but I'm starving to

death! [18]I will get up and go to my father, and say to him, "Father, I have sinned against heaven and against you. [19]I no longer deserve to be called your son. Take me on as one of your hired hands." ' [20]So he got up and went to his father.

"While he was still a long way off, his father saw him and was moved with compassion. His father ran to him, hugged him, and kissed him. [21]Then his son said, 'Father, I have sinned against heaven and against you. I no longer deserve to be called your son.' [22]But the father said to his servants, 'Quickly, bring out the best robe and put it on him! Put a ring on his finger and sandals on his feet! [23]Fetch the fattened calf and slaughter it. We must celebrate with feasting [24]because this son of mine was dead and has come back to life! He was lost and is found!' And they began to celebrate.

[25]"Now his older son was in the field. Coming in from the field, he approached the house and heard music and dancing. [26]He called one of the servants and asked what was going on. [27]The servant replied, 'Your brother has arrived, and your father has slaughtered the fattened calf because he received his son back safe and sound.' [28]Then the older son was furious and didn't want to enter in, but his father came out and begged him. [29]He answered his father, 'Look, I've served you all these years, and I never disobeyed your instruction. Yet you've never given me as much as a young goat so I could celebrate with my friends. [30]But when this son of yours returned, after gobbling up your estate on prostitutes, you slaughtered the fattened calf for him.' [31]Then his father said, 'Son, you are always with me, and everything I have is yours. [32]But we had to celebrate and be glad because this brother of yours was dead and is alive. He was lost and is found.'"

Questions

1. What are some common threads to the rebellion described in each of these Scriptures? What do they tell you about human nature?

2. How does free will play into each story? How would these stories—and our experience of the world today—be different if we did not have free will?

3. How do the characters recognize their wrongdoing in each story? What is their response to realizing their error?

4. How does God or the father figure show grace in each story? What do we learn about God through these stories?

5. Do these stories seem to illustrate prevenient (preventing) grace or justifying (conversion or being "born again") grace?

My other thoughts and questions:

Video Study and Discussion

Today's video segment features Jorge Acevedo, pastor of Grace Church, a multisite congregation with four campuses across southwest Florida. From his experience reaching out to "the people no one wants or sees," Jorge emphasizes radical hospitality and love. Wesleyan Christians acknowledge God working in every person's life, but we all have different experiences on the journey of grace.

Watch the video, then discuss the following questions:

1. Jorge quotes famous evangelist E. Stanley Jones in saying, "We do not break the Ten Commandments; we break ourselves upon them." What does this statement mean to you? What is the connection between recognizing your brokenness and experiencing God's grace?

2. What do you think of Jorge's assertion that the prodigal son's older brother was also a prodigal? What was that younger brother's sin? Which brother are you more like?

3. Do you think it is easier for the overtly rebellious people or the quiet, covertly rebellious people to experience grace in the church?

4. Jorge points out that church is a "safe place to hide" for people who don't want to show how broken they are. How can we help people be vulnerable about their brokenness, whatever their journey to grace has looked like?

5. Though church should be a safe place in which to share our brokenness, Jorge says people should expect a "dangerous" message when they hear the gospel. What is so dangerous about this message?

My other thoughts and questions:

Activity: 30-Second Testimonies

Supplies needed: kitchen timer or timer function on a watch or phone. (There is no reproducible handout for this activity.)

Some people can give a specific date and time when they experienced God's grace in a powerful way. Others have grown in understanding of God's grace over the course of many years. What is your story?

Go around the room and give each person exactly 30 seconds to tell his or her story of recognizing and accepting God's grace. If there are more than twelve to fifteen people in your class, you may wish to break into smaller groups for this activity. Enforce the 30-second limit strictly, to keep things moving and avoid one person dominating the discussion with a personal story. Afterward, briefly discuss what similarities and differences emerged across everyone's stories.

Book Study and Discussion

The book chapter we read this week looks at the Wesleyan theological understanding of grace. The discussion for the remainder of the class time should enhance participants' understanding of the Wesleyan perspective, while recognizing the value of participants' own reading of the Scriptures and experience as Christians. The passages reprinted below for your convenience should be considered references for the discussion, not an answer key for the questions provided.

1. What is prevenient grace? Do you believe people need to be aware of God's grace to experience it? How does the concept of prevenient grace affect the way you think about God's relationship with a child? a special needs person? a person who has never heard of God as we understand God?

    The journey of grace starts before we are ever aware of it. God is love, and God's love includes the whole world (John 3:16). Psalm 139 also talks about God's engagement with us even before we were born. . . .

John Wesley firmly believed that every human being is the recipient of God's grace long before we are aware of it. The word *prevenient* is not familiar today, but it is helpful in describing God's work in our lives. In Latin, *pre* means before and *veni* means "to come," so prevenient grace is God's love coming into our lives before we are aware of it.

Most Christians can point to ways in which God has been at working nudging us toward the Christian life. . . . People respond to these holy nudges in a variety of ways. Many ignore the nudges and continue life as it is. Others, sometimes after years of such promptings, finally decide to do something about it. They begin seeking God but often are unaware that it is God and faith in him for which they are looking. . . . [It's] important to remember that, because of prevenient grace, we won't be taking Christ anywhere that Christ has not already been.

2. What does it mean for someone to reject God's grace? What are some advantages and drawbacks to having free will?

A crucial part of the Wesleyan Way is the conviction that all aspects of God's grace are resistible. God created human beings in God's own image with the capacity to love each other and to love God. That requires the freedom either to love or to withhold love. Thus, God's grace can be resisted. God's offer of salvation can be refused. Despite God's best offers and best invitations, human beings can say no. God weeps when human beings reject his offer of salvation, but God loves us enough to let any one of us say no.

In their thinking about God, some Christians have put the greatest emphasis on God's power and control of the universe and all its creatures. Wesleyans do believe that God is sovereign and is ultimately in charge. We know that if God wills something, then he can make it happen to fulfill his plan. Some Christians, based on a few Bible passages that point in this direction, believe that God decided from the beginning of time which human beings should be saved and which should be excluded. They believe God worked out their destiny ahead of time, and that some were predestined to salvation and others were predestined to damnation. In this view, grace is irresistible: if God chooses to give you grace, you have no choice but to say yes.

NOTES

Those who follow the Wesleyan Way believe that God offers everyone grace and the genuine opportunity for salvation. God's sovereign power was exercised in offering salvation to every human being. This doctrine, called universal redemption, rests on the idea that Christ died for the whole world and that every person has the opportunity for salvation.

3. What different ways do people become convinced of their sin and need for grace? How is grace itself part of that convincing process?

In stanza 2 of "Amazing Grace," John Newton states it clearly: "'Twas grace that taught my heart to fear." One of the most important ways God loves us is to convince us that we need him.

If sin is a disease that disfigures the image of God in us, then convincing grace is the diagnosis that tells us what is wrong. All human beings are sinners, and all of us have issues that need to be addressed. Part of our sin is that we are very good at ignoring our problems and making excuses for our shortcomings. Convincing grace gives us a clear description of what our issues are when measured against God's expectations of us.

4. How does learning about different "types" of grace (prevenient, convincing, justifying, sanctifying) help you better understand or articulate your experience of God's grace? Do these terms complicate things for you or change in any way your description of your faith journey?

When Wesleyans talk about God's grace, we sometimes get caught up in shades of meaning determined by how people experience grace and how it changes their lives. *Prevenient* grace works in us before we are even aware of it. *Convincing* grace helps us change our ways. *Justifying* grace accepts us as part of God's family. *Sanctifying* grace changes our hearts, minds, and behaviors to be more holy. When we focus on such distinctions, we sometimes make the mistake of imagining that these types of grace are four separate things.

It's not so. Grace is grace is grace. There is just one grace of God. There is just one love of God caring for us and offering us salvation. Grace is that gift we do not deserve, offered without price because of who God is and what Christ has done for us.

Think about people who love you and what they do for you. You might be able to list their behaviors in categories that would help you distinguish ways in which they care for you and have affected your life. Yet, the overwhelming reality is simply that they love you and have given you what you needed when the time was right.

God's love is the same way.

5. How do your own experience of and understanding of God's grace affect the way you think about non-Christians? How do they affect the way you would talk about faith with non-Christians?

The New Testament makes it clear that God seeks to save every human being. Christ died for the sins of the whole world, and God is offering his grace to everyone. Wesleyans believe in universal grace. So if God loves everyone, whom should Christians love? Wesleyans believe we should love everyone God loves, which means all people.

So, if you know someone who is not a disciple of Jesus, what should you do? I am convinced that loving someone means offering to share with him or her what you have in order to meet his or her needs. We believe that everyone needs the Lord. But how are people going to find a saving relationship with Christ unless someone introduces them?

My other thoughts and questions:

Faith Stories (Optional)

There are additional short, personal video testimonies at TheWesleyanWay.com website and on your teaching DVD. You may want to spark conversation or wrap up the session the session with one of these short clips.

Scott: Grace Through Addiction (4:43)—Scott shares his difficult struggle with alcohol and prescription drug addiction and discusses how faith helped him change his life and find his own ministry helping others dealing with addiction.

5.

You Are Not Alone

Session Summary

Why would someone take up the cross? Why would someone choose to follow Jesus? Why would someone become a disciple?

The answer is grace. You are not alone. You don't have to make the journey by yourself. There are partners on the journey.

The first partner is God in the person of the Holy Spirit. The Spirit is God present with us all the time, giving us the grace we need to do what God has called us to do. The Holy Spirit is keeping us safe. In one of the worship statements used many years ago, the congregation repeated an important affirmation of faith: "In life, in death, in life beyond death, we are not alone. Thanks be to God!" There is a great sense of mystery in this. God is all-powerful and could force us to be what he intends us to be. But God is love, and God wills that we love him back and freely choose to follow the way of salvation.

There are other partners as well. The members of the church—the body of Christ—cheer us on and work alongside us. Jesus promised, "For where two or three are gathered in my name, I'm there with them" (Matthew 18:20). He promised before his death that, after he was gone, God would send another comforter to take his place and would not leave the disciples orphaned. Acts 2 describes the powerful presence of the Holy Spirit at Pentecost some fifty days after Christ's resurrection.

Christians thus believe that Christ is present in the church and that God is using the church as his primary way of accomplishing God's purposes in the world. The means of grace are the practices that God has commanded us to use in order to experience the grace he is trying to bestow upon us. Some means of grace can be practiced in solitude, but many are communal acts: baptism, Holy Communion, worship, reading Scripture, prayer, missional service and giving, and gathering in small groups for accountability and discipleship.

Before Class

It is challenging to cultivate the discipline necessary to practice all the means of grace with regularity. Before discussing the means of grace and encouraging others in these practices, take a moment to think honestly about your own practices.

1. What means of grace do you practice most regularly? Which do you tend to neglect?

2. What means of grace have you found to be most enriching to your spirit as you grow in discipleship?

Welcome

Start class with a word of greeting and prayer. Consider singing the hymn that closes the week's chapter, "Amazing Grace."

Icebreaker question: How does your church community help you grow in faith?

Bible Study and Discussion

Read the following passages from Acts 2.

Acts 2:1-21

When Pentecost Day arrived, they were all together in one place. [2]Suddenly a sound from heaven like the howling of a fierce wind filled the entire house where they were sitting. [3]They saw what seemed to be individual flames of fire alighting on each one of them. [4]They were all filled with the Holy Spirit and began to speak in other languages as the Spirit enabled them to speak.

[5]There were pious Jews from every nation under heaven living in Jerusalem. [6]When they heard this sound, a crowd gathered. They were mystified because everyone heard them speaking in their native languages. [7]They were surprised and amazed, saying, "Look, aren't all the people who are speaking Galileans, every one of them? [8]How then can each of us hear them speaking in our native language? [9]Parthians, Medes, and Elamites; as well as residents of Mesopotamia, Judea, and Cappadocia, Pontus and Asia, [10]Phrygia and Pamphylia, Egypt and the

regions of Libya bordering Cyrene; and visitors from Rome (both Jews and converts to Judaism), [11]Cretans and Arabs—we hear them declaring the mighty works of God in our own languages!" [12]They were all surprised and bewildered. Some asked each other, "What does this mean?" [13]Others jeered at them, saying, "They're full of new wine!"

[14]Peter stood with the other eleven apostles. He raised his voice and declared, "Judeans and everyone living in Jerusalem! Know this! Listen carefully to my words! [15]These people aren't drunk, as you suspect; after all, it's only nine o'clock in the morning! [16]Rather, this is what was spoken through the prophet Joel:

[17]*In the last days, God says,*
I will pour out my Spirit on all people.
   Your sons and daughters will prophesy.
   Your young will see visions.
   Your elders will dream dreams.
[18]*Even upon my servants, men and women,*
   I will pour out my Spirit in those days,
   and they will prophesy.
[19]*I will cause wonders to occur in the heavens above*
   and signs on the earth below,
   blood and fire and a cloud of smoke.
[20]*The sun will be changed into darkness,*
   and the moon will be changed into blood,
   before the great and spectacular day of the Lord comes.
[21]*And everyone who calls on the name of the Lord will be saved.*

Acts 2:41-47

Those who accepted Peter's message were baptized. God brought about three thousand people into the community on that day.

[42]The believers devoted themselves to the apostles' teaching, to the community, to their shared meals, and to their prayers. [43]A sense of awe came over everyone. God performed many wonders and signs through the apostles. [44]All the believers were united and shared everything. [45]They would sell pieces of property and possessions and distribute the proceeds to everyone who needed them. [46]Every day, they met together

NOTES

in the temple and ate in their homes. They shared food with gladness and simplicity. [47]They praised God and demonstrated God's goodness to everyone. The Lord added daily to the community those who were being saved.

Questions

1. In John 14, Jesus promises the disciples that a "Companion" (the Holy Spirit) will come to be with them after he is gone. From Acts 2, what other purposes and roles does the Spirit seem to fill?

2. If you were a devout Jew witnessing Jesus' followers speaking in many languages, what would you have thought? Would Peter's quoting of the prophet Joel have helped you make sense of what you were seeing?

3. What do you think convinced those three thousand in the crowd to accept Peter's message and be baptized?

4. Does the community of believers described in Acts 2:41-47 sound appealing to you? Why is today's church so different from that first community?

5. What means of grace do you see described in Acts 2:41-47?

My other thoughts and questions:

Video Study and Discussion

Today's video segment features Jessica Moffatt Seay, pastor of First United Methodist Church in Ardmore, Oklahoma, a big church in a small town. Jessica shares from her own family history an apt metaphor for how we experience the grace of God.

Watch the video, then discuss the following questions:

1. How does the image of God wooing you like a romantic suitor make you feel? What would God say to you in such a love letter?

2. The metaphor of faith as a marriage is an old one, from Scripture likening Israel to God's unfaithful wife to the church as the bride of Christ. What fears or challenges are there in "accepting God's proposal" and committing to new life in Christ?

3. When we consider crossing the gap between old and new life, how does God go alongside us? How can disciplines and means of grace help us cross that gap and walk through difficult times we will experience even after we are reborn?

4. How do our human companions help us on the journey? Are there any steps that must be taken alone?

5. Marriage metaphors, especially in the form of love letters, can emphasize the emotional aspects of faith. How do we walk in faith and trust God's presence even when feelings of closeness with God are not there?

My other thoughts and questions:

Activity: Means of Grace Tutorials

Supplies needed: poster paper and markers. (There is no reproducible handout for this activity.)

The means of grace are valuable practices even for lifelong Christians, but for new Christians these practices are essential to developing a deeper relationship with God and learning to feed themselves spiritually. How would you instruct a new Christian on the means of grace? Imagine the new believer asking, "Why do we do this?" "What does it mean?" and "How do I do it?" Remember that people who were not raised in church may be unfamiliar with certain "churchy" words and concepts.

Divide the class into six groups and assign each group one of the following means of grace. Give participants time to plan and write their instructions on the poster paper, then share with the group. Do any means of grace seem especially hard to explain?

Baptism
Holy Communion
Scripture and Creeds
Prayer
Small Groups
Service and Giving

Book Study and Discussion

The book chapter we read this week emphasizes the value of companionship and community in our walk with Christ. The discussion for the remainder of the class time should enhance participants' understanding of the Wesleyan perspective, while recognizing the value of participants' own reading of the Scriptures and experience as Christians. The passages reprinted below for your convenience should be considered references for the discussion, not an answer key for the questions provided.

1. Pentecost, the day when the Holy Spirit came to the disciples, is also considered to be the birthday of the church. What is the connection between the Spirit and the formation of a Christian community?

   The first partner is God, in the person of the Holy Spirit. The Spirit is God present with us all the time, giving us the grace we need to do what God has called us to do. Grace is like the harness I wore on the telephone pole. The Holy Spirit keeps us safe. . . . There are other partners on the journey. When I jumped off the pole, I was following what others had done. My group was cheering me on, letting me know they had confidence that I could do it. The church of Jesus Christ is like that.

   Jesus promised, "For where two or three are gathered in my name, I am there with them" (Matthew 18:20). He promised before his death that after he was gone, God would send another comforter to take his place and would not leave the disciples orphaned. Acts 2 describes the powerful presence of that comforter, the Holy Spirit, present at Pentecost some fifty days after Christ's resurrection, on what has been described as the church's birthday.

2. Most Christians engage in practices such as baptism, the reading of Scripture, and prayer, but referring to them as "means of grace" is a distinctly Wesleyan concept. What does this term mean, exactly, and why do we do these things?

   New Christians and others exploring the way of salvation might ask a practical question: "If God really is trying to save us, how do we get in touch with this grace you're talking about? How does the presence of the Holy Spirit really make a difference?"

John Wesley asked the same question. He knew that God is love and is actively trying to save people. He also knew that God has commanded certain practices for people to follow, and he believed that these commandments were given by God for our salvation.

They were practices that conveyed God's grace to us. . . . These means of grace are the ways in which God has promised to be present with human beings and to connect with them.

Among the means of grace provided by the church are the holy practices that God has commanded us to use. Five of these are commandments: baptism, Holy Communion, Scripture, prayer, and worship. While all of these are means of grace, the first two are sacraments because of the special significance they play in the Christian life. But all five are ways in which Christians stay in love with God.

3. Baptism and Communion are the only two practices that Wesleyans consider to be sacraments. What makes these two things special? Discuss the debates about these two sacraments and some of the differences in the way they are practiced.

For Wesleyans, there are two sacraments. Roman Catholics and others count more, but Wesleyan Christians, along with other Protestants, recognize only Holy Communion and baptism. These sacraments are outward and visible signs of an inward and spiritual grace offered by God. God is not limited to sacraments in his work, but they are reliable means by which God has promised to connect with those who faithfully partake of them. . . . Baptism is the sacrament whereby God washes away our sin and accepts us into the family of God.

The repeatable sacrament is Holy Communion. Christ commanded his disciples during the last supper he had before his crucifixion. That supper is the Passover meal that Jews eat every year to commemorate God's action in saving them from slavery in Egypt. Families traditionally eat it together, and Jesus ate it with his disciples.

Jesus transformed the Passover supper into a remembrance of his sacrifice for all humanity. . . . For generations of Christians, the sacrament of the Lord's Supper has been a powerful means of grace. In many churches this meal is called the Eucharist, because that word in Greek means "thank you." In Wesleyan practice, the pastor consecrates the elements by offering a prayer of thanksgiving to God for all that God has done. Such prayers are Trinitarian, starting by thanking God the Father, then recounting what God the Son did in the Last Supper, and then asking for the presence of the Holy Spirit in the elements that are about to be consumed.

4. Scripture, prayer, and service are three means of grace that can be done in solitude. What are the benefits of doing these things alone? What are the benefits of doing them with other believers? Which way do you prefer?

For Wesleyans, the Bible is the basic authority for our faith and practice. It is the inspired word of God that governs how we follow Christ.

Wesleyans do not teach that Scripture is infallible. Instead, we teach that the Bible contains all things necessary to salvation.

Whether one prays alone or in a congregation, silently or aloud, speaking spontaneously or reading written words, communicating with God can bring us closer to his love and his desires for our lives. . . . In 1 Thessalonians 5:17, we are told to pray without ceasing.

There are many different types of prayer.

We live in a culture that values material things and encourages us to accumulate them. We take care of ourselves and ignore the needs of others. The way of discipleship teaches the opposite: that by giving of our time, talent, and money, we will be blessed far beyond what we have given. For it is in giving away our life for the sake of the gospel that we truly find it.

5. John Wesley said, "Christianity is essentially a social religion, and that to turn it into a solitary religion is indeed to destroy it." What happens in corporate worship and small group gatherings that captures the essence of our faith? In what ways do those communal practices strengthen our faith?

It is in worship that we remind ourselves who we are and whose we are. We do that through prayer, singing, celebrating the sacraments of

Communion and baptism, and reading the Bible together. An important part of worship is preaching the word. People who have been Christians for decades have heard hundreds of sermons. A good sermon is one that faithfully communicates the message of the Bible and connects it with the life circumstances of its hearers. Many times a sermon will strike listeners as being fresh and new, even if they have heard many sermons on the same text before.

One important characteristic of early Methodism was the class meeting. To belong to the Methodist society meant attending a class in which the members watched over one another in love and helped other class members progress in the way of salvation. Members asked each other every week, "How is it with your soul?" Members told of their spiritual struggles and how they were progressing on the way of salvation.

Over time, most Wesleyans gave up the formal accountability systems of the class meeting, but Sunday school classes have picked up some of the same functions.

My other thoughts and questions:

Faith Stories (Optional)

There are additional short, personal video testimonies at TheWesleyanWay.com website and on your teaching DVD. You may want to spark conversation or wrap up the session the session with one of these short clips.

Wes: God Was With Us (2:45)—Wes Olds is interviewed by Jorge Acevedo. Wes and his wife lost their son at birth and found support from doctors, family, and friends and even a message of hope from their preschool son, Caleb.

6.

Transform Yourself and the World

Session Summary

God has a plan for your life, and that plan calls for you to grow up. No, we are not talking about chronology and being able to vote and sign contracts. We are not talking about increasing in height or weight. And we are not talking about getting married and having children or any of the other outward trappings of adulthood.

Spiritual maturity is about one's heart being transformed to become more and more like Jesus. Jesus is the model for what grown-up men and women should be like, and we want to become more like him.

The best way to describe what that looks like is to quote Jesus himself. When asked what is the greatest commandment of the law, Jesus replied in Matthew 22:37-40, "'You must love the Lord your God with all your heart, with all your being, and with all your mind.' This is the first and greatest t commandment. And the second is like it: 'You must love your neighbor as you love yourself.' All the Law and the Prophets depend on these commands." Jesus was quoting Scripture: Deuteronomy 6:5 and Leviticus 19:18. Of all the commandments in the Old Testament (and the rabbis counted more than six hundred of them), Jesus said these two were so important and so basic that all the rest hang on them.

Mature Christians love God so completely and love their neighbors as themselves so fully that everything they think, say, and do is motivated by love.

Before Class

The book chapter for today mentions several Scripture passages listing qualities toward which a mature Christian should strive (such as Matthew 5, Romans 12:9-17, 1 Corinthians 13, and Galatians 5:22-23). No one is perfect, but we do strive for lifelong improvement as our hearts grow more like that of Christ.

1. How would you rate your spiritual maturity? To use metaphors from our chronological development, are you in the terrible twos, awkward adolescence, energetic young adulthood, a midlife crisis, or wise and contented golden years?

2. What about you needs transforming? What virtues do you most strive to cultivate?

Welcome

Start class with a word of greeting and prayer. Consider singing the hymn that closes the week's chapter, "A Charge to Keep I Have."

Icebreaker question: What person whom you have known embodies, in your eyes, a mature Christian?

Bible Study and Discussion

Read the following passages from Romans 12 and Galatians 5.

Romans 12:9-18

> [9]Love should be shown without pretending. Hate evil, and hold on to what is good. [10]Love each other like the members of your family. Be the best at showing honor to each other. [11]Don't hesitate to be enthusiastic—be on fire in the Spirit as you serve the Lord! [12]Be happy in your hope, stand your ground when you're in trouble, and devote yourselves to prayer. [13]Contribute to the needs of God's people, and welcome strangers into your home. [14]Bless people who harass you—bless and don't curse them. [15]Be happy with those who are happy, and cry with those who are crying. [16]Consider everyone as equal, and don't think that you're better than anyone else. Instead, associate with people who have no status. Don't think that you're so smart. [17]Don't pay back anyone for their evil actions with evil actions, but show respect for what everyone else believes is good. [18]If possible, to the best of your ability, live at peace with all people.

Galatians 5:16-26

[16]I say be guided by the Spirit and you won't carry out your selfish desires. [17]A person's selfish desires are set against the Spirit, and the Spirit is set against one's selfish desires. They are opposed to each other, so you shouldn't do whatever you want to do. [18]But if you are being led by the Spirit, you aren't under the Law. [19]The actions that are produced by selfish motives are obvious, since they include sexual immorality, moral corruption, doing whatever feels good, [20]idolatry, drug use and casting spells, hate, fighting, obsession, losing your temper, competitive opposition, conflict, selfishness, group rivalry, [21]jealousy, drunkenness, partying, and other things like that. I warn you as I have already warned you, that those who do these kinds of things won't inherit God's kingdom.

[22]But the fruit of the Spirit is love, joy, peace, patience, kindness, goodness, faithfulness, [23]gentleness, and self-control. There is no law against things like this. [24]Those who belong to Christ Jesus have crucified self with its passions and its desires.

[25]If we live by the Spirit, let's follow the Spirit. [26]Let's not become arrogant, make each other angry, or be jealous of each other.

Questions

1. In Romans 12, Paul instructs Christians to live in a completely loving, selfless, unpretentious way. It's a very high standard. Do you believe it is possible to reach that level of spiritual maturity? How would one get to that level? How would you?

2. Paul's instructions include several examples of showing love toward those we may not naturally be inclined to: strangers, people who harass us, people of low status. Who are these people today, and how can we show love to them?

3. Paul's list of "selfish desires" in Galatians 5 includes many extreme examples that are probably not realistic temptations for most of us. Lest we skim over the whole list, take a closer look. Which vices seem most prevalent in our culture today? Which are realistic challenges for you?

4. The "fruit of the Spirit," as listed in verse 22, is not intended to correspond exactly to the list of vices in the verses above it, but we may be able to identify fruit of the

Spirit that can help us resist the temptations listed in verses 19-21. Which virtues would help us defend against which vices?

5. The fruit of the Spirit is so-called because these virtues—spiritual fruit—grow out of a heart transformed by the Spirit, the same way apples grow on an apple tree and oranges on an orange tree. How do we keep our "roots" in the Spirit pure, not to be choked out by our former self?

My other thoughts and questions:

Video Study and Discussion

Today's video segment features Felicia Hopkins, a former army chaplain and current senior associate pastor at St. Mark's United Methodist Church in El Paso, Texas. Felicia discusses how God's love transforms us into people passionate about showing love to others.

Watch the video, then discuss the following questions:

1. Felicia likens the transformation we experience in the Spirit to the changes we experience when falling in love. How does falling in love with God make us different?

2. Transformation of the heart seems useless if not directed outward to fulfill a purpose. What are two ways Felicia suggests for identifying your purpose? What other ways can you identify your calling and purpose in the world?

3. What are some of the essential truths on which all Christians are called to act?

4. Felicia says we've done a poor job of showing people that church isn't only about what happens on Sunday morning. How can we do a better job of showing people what church is about?

5. As the title of this chapter says, we must be transformed ourselves and transform the world as well. What impact does a transformed heart make on the world? Can you transform the world without a transformed heart? Can you transform it without God?

My other thoughts and questions:

Activity: Transforming Judgment into Love

Supplies needed: news articles or news video footage. If you use video, you'll need appropriate technology in the classroom. (There is no reproducible handout for this activity.)

A loving, unpretentious spirit is much harder to cultivate than it sounds. Pride and judgment come naturally to us and make us look down on people who are different from us or do things we believe are wrong. Love doesn't always wash over us like a wave of emotion—sometimes we have to be intentional about choosing to view others with love and humility.

Use your local newspaper or a news website to find a few news stories with images or video featuring people and situations that are very different from those your class participants might have experienced. Examples might include a drug bust or a shooting with mug shots, a gay pride parade, or a hate group rally. Clip or print images, or prepare to share videos you found.

Today's activity is a challenge for participants to grow in spiritual maturity by practicing the choice to love. Take a few minutes in silence to look at the people featured in these stories, imagine their struggles or motives, and try, as Paul says in Romans 12:16, to "Consider everyone as equal, and don't think that you're better than anyone else." After a few minutes of silence, allow participants to share their observations on the experience, if they so desire.

Book Study and Discussion

The book chapter we read this week focuses on growing in spiritual maturity as our hearts are transformed by the Spirit. The discussion for the remainder of the class time should enhance participants' understanding of the Wesleyan perspective, while recognizing the value of participants' own reading of the Scriptures and experience as Christians. The passages reprinted below for your convenience should be considered references for the discussion, not an answer key for the questions provided.

1. How would you define "spiritual maturity"?

Spiritual maturity is about your heart being transformed to become more and more like Jesus. Jesus is the model for what grown-up men and women should be like, and we want to become more like him.

The best way to describe that model is to quote Jesus himself. When asked the greatest commandment of the law, Jesus replied in Matthew 22:37-40, "You must love the Lord your God with all your heart, with all your being, and with all your mind. This is the first and greatest commandment. And the second is like it: You must love your neighbor as you love yourself. All the Law and the Prophets depend on these two commands." The goal of Christians is to love God so completely and love their neighbors as themselves so fully that everything they think, say, and do is motivated by love.

2. Jesus' descriptions of true holiness turned typical understandings on their heads. What perceptions of goodness do we have in the church or our culture that would be taken to a different level if we were truly transformed? Try to come up with a few "You have heard it said . . . " statements, and imagine how Jesus might reword his statements today.

Jesus' Sermon on the Mount, found in Matthew 5–7, gives several powerful descriptions of the Christian life. He began by saying that several different groups of people are blessed: the poor in spirit, those who mourn, the meek, those who hunger and thirst for righteousness, the merciful, the pure in heart, the peacemakers, and those who are persecuted for Christ's sake. John Wesley translated the Greek word *makarios* as "happy" instead of "blessed," pointing to the Wesleyan belief that those who do God's will find fulfillment, joy, and deep happiness in this life and in the world to come.

Jesus went on to quote several Old Testament laws and raise them to a new, spiritual level. For example, he cited "Don't commit murder" and then carried it further: "Everyone who is angry with their brother or sister will be in danger of judgment. If they say to their brother or sister, 'You idiot,' they will be in danger of being condemned by the governing council. And if they say, 'You fool,' they will be in danger of fiery hell" (Matthew 5:22). He cited "Don't commit adultery" and extended it: "But I say to you that every man who looks at a woman lustfully has already committed adultery in his heart" (Matthew 5:28).

3. Jesus broke down barriers by refusing to pass judgment on those whom society thought of as outcasts or sinners. How does the transformation of our hearts affect the way we judge others? Does it also change the way we judge ourselves?

But there's more to the goal of Christian life than transforming your heart and behavior. There are the larger issues of evil and immorality in our communities and nations, and Christians are called to address them.

The basis for this way of thinking about big issues is the boundary-crossing nature of Jesus' ministry. Over and over, Jesus broke the socially exclusive norms of his culture to build relationships with those considered outcasts by the Jews. He spoke with a Samaritan woman at Jacob's well (John 4:5-41). When walking through Jericho, he spoke directly to a tax collector named Zacchaeus, then ate a meal with Zacchaeus and led him to make restitution to those he had wronged (Luke 19:1-10). Jesus spoke with a Roman centurion and healed his servant (Matthew 8:5-13). He healed the daughter of a Syrophoenician woman (Mark 7:24-30). In all these circumstances, Jewish practice was to seek righteousness by avoiding sinners and outcasts such as these people. Instead, Jesus reached out to them, met their needs, and included them in his ministry.

4. The command not to judge those different from us also applies to judging other believers who may understand or apply Jesus' teachings differently. How should we approach other Christians with whom we have strong disagreements about morality, politics, or social issues?

Christians must bring their best judgment to bear on these problems [slavery, alcohol abuse, war, poverty, etc.], and more so that biblical values can be applied in all sectors of all societies throughout the world.

Yet, precisely because the problems are complex, Christians of good character and equal commitment to Christ will have disagreements. In some cases we won't prioritize problems in the same way; in other cases, we will address the same problems in radically different ways. I have often made the point that George W. Bush and Hilary Rodham Clinton are both active and faithful United Methodist Christians, and yet they belong to different political parties and have different understandings about applying Christian faith in the world.

One of the hallmarks of Wesleyan Christianity has been our ability to focus on the most important things while respecting disagreements on matters of opinion. John Wesley's sermon "Catholic Spirit" should be mandatory reading for anyone with strong opinions about theological and political matters. In that sermon, Wesley says that essential truths are different from matters of opinion. . . . Wesley's view of Catholic Spirit included the idea that on matters of opinion, it is important to realize that one's own view might be wrong. He urged people to think carefully about important issues, because it does matter what you think and how you respond. But if you know there is a chance—however small—that you might be wrong, then you must approach those who disagree in a more charitable spirit.

5. Wesley described the process of spiritual maturity (sanctification), as "going on to perfection," in keeping with Christ's command to "be perfect, as your heavenly father is perfect" (Matthew 5:48 NRSV). Can we truly be perfect? What did Wesley mean?

A key to this understanding is to realize that Matthew 5:48 has a double meaning. When Jesus said to "be perfect," his words could be translated as a prediction of the future: "you will be perfect." John Wesley believed that every commandment in Scripture is a hidden promise: What God expects us to do and be, he enables us to do and be by his grace. God's grace is constantly working in us to help transform our minds and lives.

The church is not made up of fully sanctified persons who have achieved spiritual maturity and can call themselves perfect. Rather, the church is a body of people who have committed to journeying toward that holiness. Each Christian is a sinner who needs God's grace. By the grace of God, we are making progress as individuals and groups toward the goal of holiness.

My other thoughts and questions:

Faith Stories (Optional)

There are additional short, personal video testimonies at TheWesleyanWay.com website and on your teaching DVD. You may want to spark conversation or wrap up the session the session with one of these short clips.

Rob: A Deeper Faith (4:45)—If you didn't present this video in week 3, Rob's story after experiencing a heart attack in Sunday worship could add to your discussion time. His health scare led him to deeper questions about faith and purpose.

7.

Invite Others on the Journey

Session Summary

Following Christ involves a paradox: if you want to find your life, you have to lose it for God. If you want to get the ultimate happiness, you have to give your life away to God. Those who are grasping and seeking to gain things for their own benefit will lose what they ultimately are seeking.

A Christian's blessings from God have the purpose of being a blessing for others. This theme runs throughout the Bible, starting with the call of Abraham in Genesis. God says to Abram, "Leave your land, your family, and your father's household for the land that I will show you. I will make of you a great nation and will bless you. I will make your name respected, and you will be a blessing. I will bless those who bless you, those who curse you I will curse; all the families of earth will be blessed because of you" (Genesis 12:1-3). Throughout the Old Testament, God requires Israel to take care of the widows, orphans, and aliens in their midst. The New Testament continues this message and focuses even more strongly on a life of sacrificial love.

Following Christ involves another paradox: whatever a Christian does is not the whole story. Even if you add up all the Christians in the world and what they do for God, the sum does not equal the whole story. We believe that God is the one at work in the world, through grace, to save the creation and make it the way God originally intended. Thus, giving away your life for God is often described as being a witness to God's amazing grace. The risen Christ spoke to the disciples right before his ascension: "You will receive power when the Holy Spirit has come upon you; and you will be my witnesses in Jerusalem, in all Judea and Samaria, and to the ends of the earth" (Acts 1:8).

Before Class

Evangelism can be a difficult topic for many people to talk about, precisely because their faith is hard for them to talk about! Think about your own thoughts and anxieties about evangelism before class.

1. Do you find it easy or difficult to talk about your faith? How do you tend to approach the subject when you do?

2. Do you believe that all people need to know Christ?

Welcome

Start class with a word of greeting and prayer. Consider singing the hymn that closes the week's chapter, "Come Sinners to the Gospel Feast."

Icebreaker question: As the saying goes, we are blessed to be a blessing. How have you used a blessing in your life (whether the blessing is material, spiritual, or intangible in another way) to bless others?

(Examples might include using an unexpected bonus or inheritance to make a special gift to a charity, or using one's talent for languages to teach classes in English as a second language.)

Bible Study and Discussion

Read the following passages from Matthew 28 and Mark 8.

Matthew 28:16-20

[16]Now the eleven disciples went to Galilee, to the mountain where Jesus told them to go. [17]When they saw him, they worshipped him, but some doubted. [18]Jesus came near and spoke to them, "I've received all authority in heaven and on earth. [19]Therefore, go and make disciples of all nations, baptizing them in the name of the Father and of the Son and of the Holy Spirit, [20]teaching them to obey everything that I've commanded you. Look, I myself will be with you every day until the end of this present age."

Mark 8: 31-38

³¹Then Jesus began to teach his disciples: "The Human One must suffer many things and be rejected by the elders, chief priests, and the legal experts, and be killed, and then, after three days, rise from the dead." ³²He said this plainly. But Peter took hold of Jesus and, scolding him, began to correct him. ³³Jesus turned and looked at his disciples, then sternly corrected Peter: "Get behind me, Satan. You are not thinking God's thoughts but human thoughts."

³⁴After calling the crowd together with his disciples, Jesus said to them, "All who want to come after me must say no to themselves, take up their cross, and follow me. ³⁵All who want to save their lives will lose them. But all who lose their lives because of me and because of the good news will save them. ³⁶Why would people gain the whole world but lose their lives? ³⁷What will people give in exchange for their lives? ³⁸Whoever is ashamed of me and my words in this unfaithful and sinful generation, the Human One will be ashamed of that person when he comes in the Father's glory with the holy angels."

Questions

1. What does it mean to "make disciples of all nations"?

2. Jesus responds sternly when Peter objects to the Lord's suffering. Why do you think Jesus reacts so strongly?

3. Does the idea of "losing your life" frighten you? How would you answer Jesus' questions: Why would people gain the whole world but lose their lives? What will people give in exchange for their lives?

4. With such terrifying and challenging commands as taking up one's cross and losing one's life, we can see why believers might be "ashamed" to pass on Jesus' words to others. Does this present a challenge to Jesus' call in Matthew 28:20 to teach them to "obey everything I have commanded"?

5. What are some ways in which we can overcome this fear or shame and boldly proclaim the radical message of Jesus?

My other thoughts and questions:

Video Study and Discussion

Today's video segment features Rob Fuquay, pastor of St. Luke's United Methodist Church in Indianapolis. Rob talks about the ways people come to faith and the role we can play in bringing people to Christ.

Watch the video, then discuss the following questions:

1. Displaying faith publicly can be frightening, as Rob experienced helping in worship as a youth. In what ways have you overcome fear in order to be a public witness for Christ?

2. Have you known people like the Hawaiian pastor Rob described, who came to church out of desperation when he had hit rock bottom? Have you been that person? What would you hope such a person would discover when meeting you and others in your church?

3. The Hawaiian pastor discovered God's purpose for him while cleaning toilets. Why do you think God speaks to us through such ordinary—even disgusting—things? What does that say about the call to follow Christ?

4. Evangelizing people with whom you already have a relationship can be less intimidating than evangelizing to strangers. What people whom you know already need to know God's love and purpose for their lives?

5. How can we be "live bait" rather than "artificial bait" when fishing for people? Why is authenticity so important?

My other thoughts and questions:

Activity: Inviting Conversations

Supplies needed: photocopies of the list on the next page; scissors.

Given the old adage about not discussing religion in polite company and people's common fear of public speaking, it's clear that asking people to talk about their faith may be a terrifying proposition. But it doesn't have to be so. There are many ordinary moments and solid relationships in which an opportunity for invitation can emerge naturally.

For this activity, the class should break into pairs. Each pair should receive one of the strips of paper you've cut from the following page and imagine being in the scenario described. The pair can improvise a possible conversation or simply discuss what the best tactic might be for inviting someone to Christ in such a situation. Consider what the people in each scenario might be thinking and what type of invitation would "do no harm." After five minutes, let the pairs share scenarios and their approach to evangelizing in them.

Inviting Conversations

Make a copy of this page and cut it into strips along the dotted lines. Randomly give one strip to each pair of participants. If you have more than twenty participants in the class, print more than one copy of this sheet. There is no problem in letting two groups discuss the same scenario.

Out for a walk one evening, you meet a new family that just moved in across the street.

Your close friend, who grew up religious but is no longer active in a church, is going through a difficult time and wants to have lunch.

You are reading your chapter for this Bible study on a plane, and your talkative seatmate interrupts to ask you what you're doing.

Picking your kids up from the church nursery, you strike up a conversation with a family visiting for the first time.

Your sister and brother-in-law have been raising their children without any religious instruction, and your teenage nephew shares with you his new interest in Buddhism.

A coworker complains about some aggressive evangelists who came to her door last night, and how offended she was by their assertion that she was going to hell.

Your congregation serves a free breakfast to the community every Sunday. Worship attendance isn't required, but most people do stick around, except for one guy who always eats and runs.

You volunteer at the homeless shelter with a group from your church. While there, you meet another volunteer not from your group who comes by himself to help out every Saturday.

Your best friend's daughter comes to you to confess she is now an atheist. She knows her mother will be upset, so she comes to you for advice.

Your good friend is part of another church in town, but you don't know much about it and it seems to have some strange beliefs.

Book Study and Discussion

The book chapter we read this week encourages us to have an outward-focused faith, living for others and not ourselves. Witnessing through our actions is essential, but we should not neglect witnessing with our words, which is often much harder. The discussion for the remainder of the class time should enhance participants' understanding of the Wesleyan perspective, while recognizing the value of participants' own reading of the Scriptures and experience as Christians. The passages reprinted below for your convenience should be considered references for the discussion, not an answer key for the questions provided.

1. Think about the word *witness* as we use it in a legal context. What does it mean to be a witness for Christ?

   Chapter 11 in the Book of Hebrews recounts the deeds of many people in the Old Testament, who by human measure did amazing things. But the author of Hebrews gives God the credit for what was done, because all those deeds were accomplished by faith. In two of the most powerful verses in Scripture, the author calls these persons "witnesses" saying: "So then let's also run the race that is laid out in front of us, since we have such a great cloud of witnesses surrounding us. Let's throw off any extra baggage, get rid of the sin that trips us up, and fix our eyes on Jesus, faith's pioneer and perfecter. He endured the cross, ignoring the shame, for the sake of the joy that was laid out in front of him, and sat down at the right side of God's throne." (Hebrews 12:1-2)

2. Witnessing in deed through our actions is essential as we "walk the walk" not just "talk the talk," but witnessing in our words is important as well. Do you think people need an explanation when loving actions are done in the name of Christ? What are the benefits of explaining our motives? What are the drawbacks?

   Sometimes skeptics rightly ask whether we as disciples of Jesus "walk the walk" or just "talk the talk." Even Jesus was aware of this problem, as seen in his parable of the man with two sons. (Matthew 21:28-31)

   In a similar way, the behaviors exhibited by Christians need explanation. People who look at our food pantries may not know that we are giving out food for Christ. People who watch us worship may not understand why we sing and pray and preach. People who observe us lobby

Congress for the well-being of the poor or for justice to immigrants may not see the deeper reasons of faith behind what we do.

Wesleyans believe it is God who does the saving work, and we are simply God's instruments. We are small parts of a much larger process. We owe it to God and to those we serve to proclaim and explain that process and to give God the credit. You might call it "truth in labeling." If we are helping to change the world in Christ's name, then Christ should be credited.

3. Do you believe all people need Christ? Do you believe all people need the church?

God has commanded us to love others, so if we become aware that one of our neighbors does not know Christ as Lord and Savior, we should figure out how to love that person well. Loving our neighbors means doing good to their souls as well as to their bodies.

A powerful slogan expressing that belief is: "Make a friend. Be a friend. Bring a friend to Christ." If a Christian really cares about someone and knows that the person's life would be happier and better as a disciple, then offering a relationship with Christ is the most logical and natural thing in the world.

[If] we believe that everyone needs Christ, then our course of action is clear. We should invite George and Jane to church, so they can know Christ and profess their faith in him.

Wesleyan Christians believe that George and Jane need Christ, because Christ wants to be everyone's Lord and Savior. This way of salvation is the path to happiness, fulfillment, and eternal life.

4. Evangelism means "good message." How have we sometimes turned this good news into bad news?

Invitations to church should be made lovingly and respectfully. Evangelism literally means "good message." The content of the message, in its simplest form, is that God loves you and wants a relationship to help you find fulfillment in life. To many people, that's good news.

But in two thousand years, Christians have managed to deliver the invitation in a number of ways that come across as bad news. Christians have sometimes talked about sin, damnation, and hell as the initial expression of God's love. Christians have sometimes acted with hate, racism, sexism, exclusion, and greed so that our actions contradict the goodness of the words. We have even baptized people as we put them into slavery.

5. Bringing people to Christ can take many forms: inviting people to worship, to work on a mission project, or to a private lunch for conversation. What invitation can you commit to giving in the next week?

Evangelism can be as simple as asking a friend, "Do you have a church?" If the answer is yes, it's wonderful news and there's a new bond between the two of you. If the answer is no, or "I'm looking for a church to attend," then you can invite them to yours.

Such an invitation should never be given to someone who is active in a different church. That would be like stealing sheep from another part of the same flock. Wesleyans believe that Baptists, Roman Catholics, Episcopalians, Bible church members, Presbyterians, and other kinds of Christians are all disciples of Jesus. When someone transfers from one part of the flock to another, there's no net gain for the kingdom of God.

My other thoughts and questions:

Faith Stories (Optional)

There are additional short, personal video testimonies at TheWesleyanWay.com website and on your teaching DVD. You may want to spark conversation or wrap up the session the session with one of these short clips.

Adam: Bless the Schools (4:39)—If you didn't present this video in week 2, Adam's video about Church of the Resurrection's partnership with area schools lifts up the way a congregation can show love and model Christ for the community around them.

8.

Christ No Matter What

Session Summary

· Bad things still happen to good people. Following Christ does not mean complete protection from disaster, disappointment, disease, and other bad events. Deep down, many people expect that those who follow Christ, who conduct lives guided by the highest moral values, and who actively participate in church should be rewarded in this life. They should live longer, have happier marriages, raise good children, be successful in their work, and generally be more fulfilled and better off than those who live without God and follow less ethical pathways.

Taken as a whole, people with active faith commitments—participating in a religious community and practicing the highest moral values—often do lead happier and more fulfilled lives. Yet, there are those cases in which people ask, "Why did God allow this to happen?"

Sometimes the disappointments we experience are not life-threatening. When a spouse is unfaithful and the marriage dissolves, a person can struggle with feelings of rejection, low self-esteem, and despair. Or someone might lose a job because of an economic downturn so that the income on which that person had planned is no longer flowing in, and a complete life adjustment is now in order. In these situations, some people respond to the stress of life by turning to alcohol and drugs, which further complicate their problems. Other problems truly are life-threatening: cancer diagnoses, car accidents, abusive relationships; major natural disasters such as hurricanes, tsunamis, earthquakes, and tornadoes.

The Christian response to all these problems is that we are never alone in dealing with them. Christ always journeys with us, so we can choose to respond to sorrow with faith, and keep following Christ no matter what.

Before Class

Questions about why bad things happen and what happens after this life are among the most enduring questions in all humanity. That being the focus of today's discussion, think beforehand about your own questions and anxieties.

1. How much anxiety do you experience over present struggles or possible trials and tragedies you may experience in the future?

2. How much anxiety do you experience over your own death and what comes after that? What about the death and afterlife of loved ones?

Welcome

Start class with a word of greeting and prayer. Note that for this, the last session of this study, the activity and singing of the hymn will be at the conclusion of the discussion.

Icebreaker question: How do you respond to people who have just experienced a tragedy? What do you say to them? What do you do for them?

Bible Study and Discussion

Read the following passage from Romans 8.

Romans 8:18-39

> I believe that the present suffering is nothing compared to the coming glory that is going to be revealed to us. [19]The whole creation waits breathless with anticipation for the revelation of God's sons and daughters. [20]Creation was subjected to frustration, not by its own choice—it was the choice of the one who subjected it—but in the hope [21]that the creation itself will be set free from slavery to decay and brought into the glorious freedom of God's children. [22]We know that the whole creation is groaning together and suffering labor pains up until now. [23]And it's not only the creation. We ourselves who have the Spirit as the first crop of the harvest also groan inside as we wait to be adopted and for our bodies to be set free. [24]We were saved in hope. If we see what we hope for, that isn't hope. Who hopes for what they already see? [25]But if we hope for what we don't see, we wait for it with patience.

²⁶In the same way, the Spirit comes to help our weakness. We don't know what we should pray, but the Spirit himself pleads our case with unexpressed groans. ²⁷The one who searches hearts knows how the Spirit thinks, because he pleads for the saints, consistent with God's will. ²⁸We know that God works all things together for good for the ones who love God, for those who are called according to his purpose. ²⁹We know this because God knew them in advance, and he decided in advance that they would be conformed to the image of his Son. That way his Son would be the first of many brothers and sisters. ³⁰Those who God decided in advance would be conformed to his Son, he also called. Those whom he called, he also made righteous. Those whom he made righteous, he also glorified.

³¹So what are we going to say about these things? If God is for us, who is against us? ³²He didn't spare his own Son but gave him up for us all. Won't he also freely give us all things with him?

³³Who will bring a charge against God's elect people? It is God who acquits them. ³⁴Who is going to convict them? It is Christ Jesus who died, even more, who was raised, and who also is at God's right side. It is Christ Jesus who also pleads our case for us.

³⁵Who will separate us from Christ's love? Will we be separated by trouble, or distress, or harassment, or famine, or nakedness, or danger, or sword? ³⁶As it is written,

> We are being put to death all day long for your sake.
> We are treated like sheep for slaughter.

³⁷But in all these things we win a sweeping victory through the one who loved us. ³⁸I'm convinced that nothing can separate us from God's love in Christ Jesus our Lord: not death or life, not angels or rulers, not present things or future things, not powers ³⁹or height or depth, or any other thing that is created.

Questions
1. How does focusing on "coming glory" help one to cope with "present sufferings"? Do you think this approach is helpful for everyone?

NOTES

2. Note the apocalyptic implications of verses 22-23. Is hope of imminent glory through rapture or apocalypse helpful?

3. What is the power of praying through "unexpressed groans"? How does the Spirit help us pray?

4. What does verse 28 mean to you? How all-encompassing is this promise? Does it mean that God knows and wills everything that happens?

5. How does the promise that nothing can separate us from the love of God, even in death, apply to our ideas about hell and eternal punishment?

My other thoughts and questions:

Video Study and Discussion

Today's video segment features Scott J. Jones, bishop of the United Methodist Church in Kansas and Nebraska and author of *The Wesleyan Way*. Scott talks about how, in a sometimes confusing and challenging world, God and God's church are forces for hope and good.

Watch the video, then discuss the following questions:
1. Scott says that he went into ministry because he believed the church was the best tool for social change. Do you agree? Are we leading the kind and amount of social change that we are capable of making?

2. There is a big difference between membership and discipleship. How would you describe that difference? Does your congregation have high expectations of its members? Should it?

3. Scott describes the Wesleyan Way as part of the "extreme center." What does this term mean to you? Do you think others understand this position in the range of religious traditions? How can we show others the value of the extreme center?

4. How do we live out and share our unique way of following God, while humbly respecting the wide range of Christian and non-Christian traditions?

5. How does the promise that "all things work together for good for those who love God" (Romans 8: 28 NRSV) help us deal with the many unknowns in life? How does this promise fit with our belief in human free will?

My other thoughts and questions:

Book Study and Discussion

The book chapter we read this week expresses the basis for our hope, in spite of the tragedies and sorrows of life, the unknowns of life and death, and the mystery of what the Bible refers to as "the last days." The discussion for the remainder of the class time should enhance participants' understanding of the Wesleyan perspective, while recognizing the value of participants' own reading of the Scriptures and experience as Christians. The passages reprinted below for your convenience should be considered references for the discussion, not an answer key for the questions provided.

1. We believe that God knows more than we do and that God's ways are "higher" than our ways. Does that mean that some suffering might be part of God's plan?

   We human beings are impatient and want to learn more of what God knows. In the story of Job, he asked God the question *Why?* and at a crucial point in the story, God replied:

   "Who is this darkening counsel with words lacking knowledge? Prepare yourself like a man; I will interrogate you, and you will respond to me. Where were you when I laid earth's foundations? Tell me if you know. Who set its measurements? Surely you know. Who stretched a measuring tape on it? On what were its footings sunk; who laid its cornerstone, while the morning stars sang in unison and all the divine beings shouted?" (Job 38:2-7)

   God was basically saying, "Who are you to question my ways?" As much as we long to know why, there are some things we will never know in this life, and when we get to heaven, as the man in my congregation said, it truly won't matter.

2. How does faith in God help us endure suffering? Is the extent to which our faith helps us an indicator of spiritual maturity?

The image of God preparing a table for us to dine in the presence of our enemies is a powerful metaphor for how God can bless us in the midst of our troubles. Many times I have heard people in the midst of great difficulties—even in the process of dying—talk about how Christ was comforting them and how their faith was getting them through the hard times.

When people who are suffering can experience the love and grace of God, they can see a way forward to overcome the hard times. The crucial element in such a situation is how people respond. They can reject God's grace and allow the suffering to overwhelm them, or they can respond with faith and allow God's grace maximum space to work.

3. Do you believe—whether through Scripture, Christian doctrine, or popular testimonies of those who have had near-death experiences—that we can know for certain what awaits us after death? Does certainty give you comfort? Does uncertainty cause you anxiety, or are you comfortable with uncertainty?

Two key scriptural texts have shaped Christian thinking about life after death. First, Jesus engaged in a conversation with the two criminals who were crucified with him. One cursed Jesus, and the other defended him, maintaining that Jesus was innocent and saying, "Remember me when you come into your kingdom." Jesus replied, "I assure you that today you will be with me in paradise" (Luke 23:43).

A few years later Paul wrote to the church at Corinth:

Listen, I'm telling you a secret: all of us won't die, but we will all be changed—in an instant, in the blink of an eye, at the final trumpet. The trumpet will blast, and the dead will be raised with bodies that won't decay, and we will be changed. (1 Corinthians 15:51-57)

4. The Wesleyan Way asserts that all people, regardless of creed or culture, have been given prevenient grace, and that God will not condemn anyone without a realistic opportunity for salvation. In your mind, what would constitute a "realistic opportunity"? What would it take for someone to be condemned to eternal punishment?

Wesleyans understand that everyone has received sufficient grace from God to be saved. The question, then, is whether we choose to use the grace God has provided. John Wesley said, "No man sins because he has not grace, but because he does not use the grace which he hath." (*The Works of John Wesley*, ed. by W. Reginald Ward and Richard J. Heitzenrater; Abingdon Press, 2005; 3:207)

Within the list of God's attributes, we count on God to know everything, to love everyone, to be righteous, and to be faithful for all time. Wesleyans believe that God loves us and allows us the free will to reject his love. Thus, whatever happens to us in eternity is a result of how we have responded to God's grace in this life.

We cannot know any particular person's state of salvation. God alone knows the heart of that person and will always judge fairly and correctly.

5. With so much we cannot know—reasons why bad things happen; specifics about heaven, hell, and salvation; details about end-times—how do we face life and death confidently? How do we follow Christ boldly when there is so much uncertainty?

One of the most important scriptural texts about predicting the end of the world comes from Jesus. After describing some of the signs, he said in Matthew 24:36, "But nobody knows when that day or hour will come, not the heavenly angels and not the Son. Only the Father knows." Based on this text, not even Jesus while he was on earth knew when these things would happen.

Whatever happens in our lives, the fundamental principle that guides discipleship is to follow Christ in everything we think, say, and do. The triune God is the ultimate reality of the universe, and God has created each of us for a purpose—to love God and neighbor in everything.

We do so in community. Christ saves individuals, but salvation always involves being formed into the body of Christ, which is the church. The church has taken different forms at various points in history, but whatever form it has taken, participation in the gathered community of believers has never been optional.

My other thoughts and questions:

Faith Stories (Optional)

There are additional short, personal video testimonies at TheWesleyanWay.com website and on your teaching DVD. You may want to spark conversation or wrap up the session the session with one of these short clips.

Amy: Not Broken But Broken Open (5:25)—Amy's son was born prematurely; though she and her husband were assured he was in good health, an unexpected infection took his life. In this very emotional testimony, Amy tells us how her faith carried them through grief.

Activity: "No Matter What" Prayer Experience

Supplies needed: watch or clock with a second hand. Optional: candle and matches or lighter. (There is no reproducible handout for this activity.)

Wrap up the book discussion with five minutes to spare before the end of your class time. Let the class know you are moving into a time of prayer, and consider lighting a candle to symbolize Christ's presence among you. Say the following:

As we conclude today's discussion and this study of the Wesleyan Way, let us meditate on the words that make up the title of today's chapter: "Christ, no matter what." Take a moment to get comfortable, and let Christ come in to whatever fear, grief, or struggle you may be facing, or whatever anxiety about struggles you may face in the future. Christ is Lord and will be with us, no matter what. Let us pray in silence.

Inconspicuously keep your eye on your clock or watch, so that every thirty seconds or so, for a total of four or five minutes, you can repeat the focus phrase: *Christ, no matter what.*

Close with: *Let's all say it together: Christ, no matter what. Amen.*

End class by singing together Charles Wesley's hymn, "Christ the Lord Is Risen Today."